ANCIENT AMERICAN INDIANS

ANCIENT AMERICAN INDIANS

Paul R. Cheesman
Millie F. Cheesman

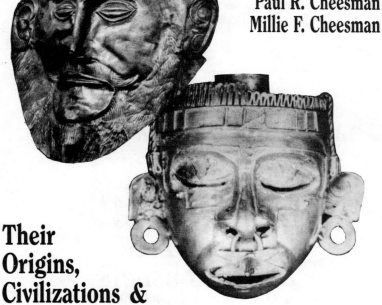

Their Origins, Civilizations & Old World Connections

First Printing: October 1991

International Standard Book Number
0-88290-416-7

Horizon Publishers' Catalog and Order Number
2004

Printed and distributed
in the United States of America by

Horizon
Publishers
& Distributors, Incorporated
P.O. Box 490 Bountiful, Utah 84011-0490

Dedication

The book is dedicated to the memory of President Spencer W. Kimball, who encouraged me in this project, becasue of his great love and respect for the Indians as a chosen race.

A special thanks to Phil Buchanan, who accompanied and assisted me on some of my research trips.

Deepest appreciation is expressed to Lillian M. Wilbur for her invaluable help in putting together the finished manuscript. Also, thanks to D. Lee Walker for his help as my assistant.

And finally, I extend heartfelt appreciation to my wife, Millie, who has accompanied me on my research trips and helped me complete this complicated manuscript.

Introduction

For over twenty years the author has gathered information for this publication, ending with his latest study on the cultural similarities between the Old and New Worlds. After reading many hundreds of books, traveling thousands of miles in over 30 research trips, taking eight thousand photographs and slides, and preparing numerous maps and charts as visual resources, he is offering this study on three related subjects:

1. the origins of the American Indians,
2. cultural parallels between the Old and the New World, and
3. temples, mounds, and ruins in prehistoric North America.

Since Dr. Cheesman's entire adult life has been devoted to the study of pre-Columbian peoples of the Americas, he has enjoyed relating this information to Christian studies, particularly as it pertains to ancient New World records. The author hopes this particular study might enlarge the reader's understanding of these ancient people, even bringing feelings of admiration for their talent, intelligence and skills. Perhaps this data might help him also to present the American Indians in a new light—with even more understanding and respect for their royal lineage and marvelous destiny as a unique people.

Contents

PART ONE

CONTENTS

Page

PART TWO

Photographic Comparisons of Old and New World Parallels

Part One

1

Ancient North American Cultures

In the ongoing study of ancient American cultures, the main emphasis in the past has been with the civilizations of Mexico, and Central and South America, because of the abundance of study-material from ancient ruins and burial sites. For centuries scholars have been drawn, almost as if by magnet-force, to those ancient lands with their imposing pyramids, their art and their priceless treasures. Libraries are filled with books telling of mysterious cultures which existed in America, long before Columbus landed upon these shores in the fifteenth century.

The author is of the opinion that students and scholars have neglected the studies of North American Indian cultures before the Spanish conquest. Some have believed North America had little to offer regarding ancient American studies because there are no magnificent stone pyramids. Therefore, the author has devoted three years to investigative, on-site studies, in over thirty-five states, photographing and cataloging the better-known ruins and civilizations of pre-Columbian North America.

It is the author's hope, in the brief cross-cut study of this chapter, to acquaint the reader with some of the more prominent North American Indian archaeological sites and museums. Volumes could be written on this subject. Therefore, suffice it to say, the information and descriptions will, of necessity, be brief. It may even surprise the reader to learn that the foundation of one of the largest pre-Columbian ruins in the Americas is found on the outskirts of St. Louis, Missouri, in the Cahokia Mounds State Park in Collinsville, Illinois. Having visited this lost Indian civilization, the author became fascinated with what appears to be the largest and most powerful American Indian civilization north of Mexico. Known as Monk's Mound, it is the largest prehistoric construction north of the Temple of the Sun at Teotihuacan, Mexico, dating back to A.D. 750 (Late Woodland)[1]

The Eight Major Early Tribal Groups

The author wishes to present this study in eight major areas of North America, noting the similarities and differences according to general geographic locations. The following are the eight major *early* tribes, with a map indicating their general habitat:

1. *Eastern Woodland Area*
   Types: Pee dee, Adena, Hopewell, Shawnee
2. *Southeastern Area*
   Types: Cherokee, Tookabalchas, Creek
3. *Plains Area*
   Types: Wichita, Caddo, Kiowa, Mandan, Pawnee
4. *Southwest Area*
   Types: Navajo, Apache, Pima, Hopi, Anasazi, Pueblo
5. *California Area*
   Types: Pomo, Chumash, Salish, Yuma
6. *Plateau Area*
   Types: Nez Perce, Walla Walla, Palouse, Spokane
7. *North Pacific Coast Area*
   Types: Nootka
8. *Great Basin Area*
   Types: Ute, Paiute

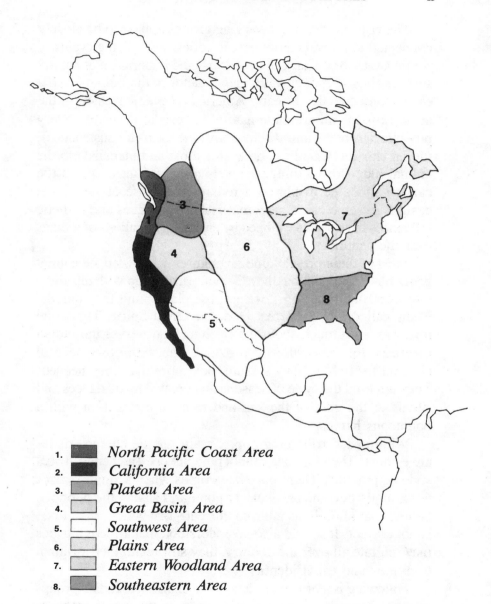

1. North Pacific Coast Area
2. California Area
3. Plateau Area
4. Great Basin Area
5. Southwest Area
6. Plains Area
7. Eastern Woodland Area
8. Southeastern Area

The rise and fall of the varying groups appear to be closely connected to (1) wars amongst the tribes, and (2) the cycles of nature (water or the lack of it). Clearly the importance of natural surroundings certainly was a prime factor in the Indians' existence. Consequently, the early Americans became masters of the art of utilizing all available natural materials, as well as every possible part of the animal kingdom—the meat (for sustenance), the fat (for fuel), and the bone (for tools and utensils), to the animal hide (for clothing, blankets and dwellings). From the earliest times he displayed a remarkable sense of functional design. In some cases, new materials, techniques and esthetic influences have been developed by ensuing generations of Indians over the centuries.

Most of these pre-Columbian cultures acknowledged a great godly power and felt that they lived in partnership with this diety who controlled the sun, the rain, the plants, and the animals. Many called him the Great God, the Great Spirit. The white man can learn much about the earth as he observes the Indian reverence for the earth as it provides man with every needful element for living. They seldom took more than they needed. They honored the cycle of seasons and created many dances and rituals to the gold of the sun and rain, in connection with a bounteous harvest.

Within each tribe or group, certain unique characteristics are evident. Therefore one cannot pinpoint one "authentic" tribal style or practice. There have been times when a single artist's work might become particularly popular, causing the public to believe that all Indians fall into this category which, of course, is not correct. It should also be understood that although tribes may migrate all over the country, they still retain their original traditions and tribal identity.

Following is a brief overview of the eight basic Indian groups in early America, as preserved in some of the major archaeological areas of North America:

EASTERN WOODLAND AREA

Town Creek Indian Mound
(Mount Gilead, North Carolina)

This culture is given the name of "Pee Dee," taken from the name of the basin in which they lived. Although Indians came to North Carolina many years before Christ, the Town Creek Mound Indians were a much later group who were found by the early European settlers. This tribal ceremonial center has been excavated and rebuilt, with the ancient temple atop the mound and the priests' house restored by Mr. Stanley A. South, archaeologist for the North Carolina State Department of Archives and history.

This center contained a temple, with a series of burial houses enclosed within a palisade of upright logs. Numerous Indian villages were scattered along the Pee Dee River, consisting of dome-shaped straw-covered huts. Women dominated village life, for this society named their descendants through the female line. The wife's family owned the property; the husband lived in the house of the wife's family, along with their children and the wife's blood relatives. Women tended to most of the village chores, cared for the children and made clothing, blankets and pottery. They pounded corn into meal, wove mats, baskets, split cane and worked in the fields. The men were responsible for clearing the fields and building huts, canoes, drums, tools, weapons and wooden mortars for grinding corn.[2]

They were farmers who had a unique ability to make the land productive, and they also held to some distinctive customs. Arriving in the 15th century, they brought with them their religious ideas, building habits, ceremonial practices and even a game called "chunkey." They lived here for about 200 years and departed in the 17th century, due to warring with their neighbors.[3]

This is one of the few North American sites that has been restored, with replicas of original temples and ceremonial centers, so it is particularly interesting.

Town Creek Mounds, Pee Dee culture,
Mt. Gilead, North Carolina.

The Grave Creek or Mammouth Mound
(Moundsville, West Virginia)

The world-famous Mammoth Indian burial mound, known to archaeologists as the Grave Creek Mound, is the chief attraction of the city of Moundsville, West Virginia. This area, known as the Ohio Valley, was inhabited by the Adena culture about four thousand years before Christ (late Archaic). When it was discovered in 1938, it stood 69 feet high and ended with a flat top 60 feet in diameter and was surrounded by a circular ditch. It was only one of 100 such mounds built in the centuries which followed, many of which were used as burial places for important people. All but the one remaining mound have been destroyed by modern industrial expansion.

One of the more interesting aspects of this site involves a small oval tablet called the Grave Creek Stone, discovered by A.B. Tomlinson in 1938, within one of the Adena burial mounds built about A.D. 1. This little greyish sandstone tablet measured about 1½x2 inches, with markings believed to be an undecipherable language. There are twenty-two characters, with one repeated three times and another twice. There was considerable controversy over the stone, but some scholars have classified the writing as European. The translations were varied and dissimilar—some with religious implications. This stone has since been lost, but not before the Smithsonian Institution made a cast of it and a careful account was recorded by Dr. William C. Mills in 1839. Later Mr. Delf Norona, Director of the Museum, researched this and other accounts of the find and put the stories together in a booklet entitled *Moundsville's Mammoth Mound.*[4] There is still great controversy over this stone, but the author presents this information as a matter of interest, encouraging the reader to keep an open mind. Perhaps future studies may shed new light on the archaic writing.

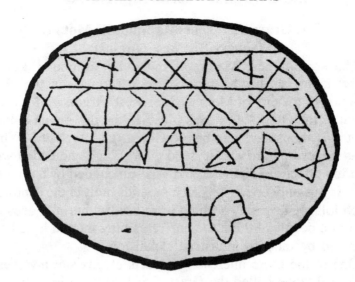

Grave Creek Stone, undecipherable
language, circa A.D. 100

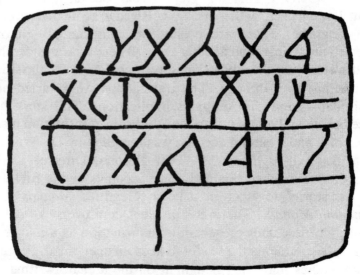

The Wilson Tablet, markings similar
to Grave Creek Stone,
Braxton County, West Virginia

Grave Creek or Mammoth Mound, late archaic, circa 3000 B.C., Moundsville, West Virginia.

The Larkin Tablets

When a mound was destroyed on the home property of Everett N. Swartze, of Mason County, West Virginia, two inscribed tablets were found—now known as The Larkin Tablets. The backs of both tablets (measuring about 2¾x3⅛ inches) were smooth and were found with eight projectile points (used for writing), two lumps of black graphite and a white cone. Pencil rubbings were made for study by the West Virginia Archaeological Society, and later Mr. Swartze brought the tablets to the Society. Both stones appear to bear abstract markings very similar to numberless Mayan pictoglyphs found on artifacts from ancient Mexico. The Society's continued studies on these stones are helping to diminish the suspicions regarding other similar discoveries.[5]

 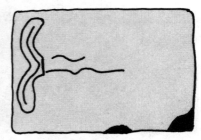

The Larkin Tablet, marking similar to Mayan Pictoglyphs, from mound owned by Everett N. Swartz, Mason County, West Virginia (Drawings after Edward V. McMichael, Introduction to West Virginia Archaeology.[6])

The Wilson Tablet

The Wilson Tablet was found by Blaine Wilson on April 10, 1921, in Braxton County, West Virginia, 8 miles west of Gassaway on Triplett Creek—the right-hand fork of Steer Creek. The markings on this stone are very similar to the ones on the Grave Creek Stone. Naturally, there is controversy over the Wilson Tablet, also, in that they are much alike in their style of glyphs. The characters or symbols are considered to be Phoenician, Libyan, Celtiberic, and Runic (Norse). But, time and study may be on the side of their authenticity. An interesting quote comes from one Mr. James Ralston Skinner, who made a careful study of the American mounds, relating the discovery of 2 stones in Newark, Ohio, which were covered with "Old Hebrew inscriptions." After being examined by "competent judges" they were pronounced to be of great antiquity. And yet, due to their being discovered by a lay person (Mr. Wyrick), in an uncontrolled situation, they were declared doubtful. J.R. Skinner's response to this is interesting regarding archaic stone tablets in the New World.

Now, as sustaining his veracity, it is to be seen that there is this very curious combination of data, with respect to these mounds: The mounds are monumented circles and squares, or relations of circular and right line measure. To these the Egyptians and the Hebrews, alike, were addicted, in the workings of their highest religious cultus. Both Egyptians and Hebrews seem to have derived their knowledge from the common source of the Phoenician. The great pyramid monumenting this cultus stands on the West bank of the Nile, the side of sculpture. The books of the Egyptians containing this knowledge were called *the books of the dead.*[7]

It is the author's opinion that whenever there are discoveries which might possess even the slightest religious overtones, some scholars brand the research as fraudulent, simply to protect their academic reputations.

Both of these stone tablet sets of two are found in the Museum at Moundsville, West Virginia, where a placard explains how "...archaeologists from Pittsburgh's Carnegie Museum have stated that Indians roamed the Valley of Ohio in Hancock County 3000 years ago...[indicating] the Archaic or pre-pottery period."[8]

Paleo Indian and Archaic Period

The Paleo Indian period is thus named because they were believed to be the first Indian culture to roam the area of the Ohio Valley. This period is characterized by the use of peculiarly grooved projectile points on their weapons. They were basically hunters.

The Archaic period follows the Paleo Indian culture. It is also considered a non-agricultural group. The Indians of this time period lived by hunting, fishing, and gathering of natural foods. They did not make pottery, but developed needles, harpoons and a weapon called the atlatl, which allowed them to throw a spear much farther and more accurately. The polished stone tools first appeared in their culture.

The Hopewell Adena Culture
(Archaic Period)

The Hopewell Adena culture was a well organized tribe living in a wide area of the Ohio Valley, West Virginia, Indiana, Kentucky, parts of western Pennsylvania and New York. They were larger in stature than their ancestors and quite progressive in their way of life. They were the first of the known Indian groups to practice agriculture.

Their villages appear to be organized on the basis of extended family tribes. Of all the prehistoric societies inhabiting the Ohio Valley, the Hopewell were the most skillful in making elaborate artifacts, complex earthworks and burial mounds. Some scholars are of the opinion they may have migrated to the Ohio Valley from Mexico.

Migrations from the south into the north countries certainly were not an impossibility. The pre-Columbian garbage dumps in North America indicate trade and communication with the people southward, with recognizable pottery styles from those areas appearing in the "trash" studied by modern archaeologists.

Mound City
(Chillicothe, Ohio)

By approximately 300 B.C., the prehistoric Indians we now classify as Hopewell had developed a rather sophisticated culture in the Middle West. For approximately 900 years they flourished, with the apex of their culture being in the Scioto Valley of southern Ohio. They were best known for their artistic achievements in metalcraft, stone carvings, jewelry and pottery. It appears they practiced simple agriculture and were a peaceful people.

This site was mapped and partially excavated in 1846 by two archaeologists, E.G. Squier and E.H. Davis, resulting in a publication by the Smithsonian Institution in the same year. This study produced some spectacular artifacts which were eventually

Mound City, 300 B.C., Hopewell, Chillicothe, Ohio.

acquired by the British Museum in London where they remain to this day. However, in 1920-21 the Ohio Historical society sponsored further excavation, and much of their material is on exhibit at the Mound City Visitors' center and the Ohio Historical Center. Recent excavation in 1963 has resulted in an improved restoration of the site, providing a great storehouse of information about the Hopewell culture.

Dating back 1800 years, this "city of graves" was believed to be a ceremonial center for the dead, particularly their honored leaders. It was possibly the most spectacular Indian site in North America. These dirt mounds were created to cover the cremated remains of their honored dead with a wooden structure used for the last rites. This site covers 13 acres, within which are 23 burial mounds. One is a pottery mound, from which archaeologists were able to preserve beautiful examples of their highly developed ceramic art.[9]

The Moses Stone
(Coshocton, Ohio)

In a small museum in Coshocton, Ohio is a black stone measuring three inches by two inches by eight inches. Found in 1860, in a stone box near a human skeleton,[10] some twenty feet below the surface of a mound near Newark, Ohio, it is dated from 200 B.C. to A.D. 300.[11] On one side a face of a man is carved in relief with the inscription, *"Mose"* (the Hebrew version of the name Moses). And, appropriately enough, around the stone the Ten Commandments are inscribed. Some have called the Newark or Moses Stone a hoax.[12] However, the letters are not like modern Hebrew letters, but are ancient in style—similar to both the old Phoenician and the later South Arabic script. The ancient shaping of letters on the Moses Stone does present a problem for those who cry, "Hoax," in that the South Arabic script was not actually studied until late in the 19th century.[13]

The Moses or Newark Stone, the box in which it was found, and the key stone, 200 B.C.–A.D., Coshocton, Ohio.

Along with the Moses Stone was a different type of rock bearing Hebrew inscriptions as well, called the "Key Stone." This was, on occasion, used as proof of the antiquity on the Masonic Order because the key is an important symbol in Masonry belief. Unfortunately, the Hebrew letters on the Key Stone are modern and therefore considered fraudulent by scholars. Again, the author presents this information as a matter of interest.

The Serpent Mound
(Near Locust Grove, Ohio)

This gigantic serpent in the act of uncoiling is considered the largest known serpent effigy in the world. Lying on top of a curved spur of land one hundred feet above and leading into the valley of Brush Creek, this cresent-shaped elevation symbolzed the serpent to the prehistoric inhabitants of the region. The entire earthwork follows the shape of the land spur on which it lies. Within the open jaws of the serpent is an oval wall of earth thought to represent an egg which the serpent is in the process of swallowing. The length of the serpent from head to tail is 1,254 feet, with the average width of the body being about twenty feet. There is a burial mound and a housing site nearby, along with implements of stone, bone and copper.

The first careful survey of this area was made by Ephraim G. Squier and Edwin H. Davis, with a report published in 1848 entitled *Ancient Monuments of the Mississippi Valley*. Then Frederic W. Putnam of Harvard University visited the mound in 1886, resulting in the present restoration, following Squier and Davis' drawings.

The Serpent Mound symbolized to the builders, no doubt, some religious principle. In view of its size and construction, the mound was extremely important to the Adenas.

Serpent Mound, prehistoric, largest known serpent effigy in the world, near Locust Grove, Ohio.

The serpent has played an important part in world religions. For many people the serpent symbolized eternity, apparently because of a serpent's ability to shed its skin and thereby renew its life. For others it represents evil, as in the Garden of Eden and the story of the creation in the book of Genesis. (See Genesis 3:1.) Among the Greeks the serpent was the symbol of healing diety, *Asklepios*. The serpent of the Mayas was held in great reverence, appearing prominently on their ancient temples and pyramids. The serpent carvings on stone among the Indians of the Mississippi Valley and the Snake Dance of the Hopi are other examples of the importance of the serpent symbol in North American cultures. Even today, two intertwined serpents constitute the logo of the medical profession.

Some Hopis believe this Serpent Mound may have been constructed by their ancestors. Trenches dug throughout the effigy reveal a core of clay and stone, implying the shape of the serpent was carefully planned before construction. During the official excavation, the conical mound measured nine feet in height and seventy feet in diameter. Artifacts indicate that the mound was built by the pre-historic Adena Indians, who lived in Ohio between 1000 B.C. and A.D. 200. Because of this mound's proximity to the Effigy Mound (Davenport, Iowa), archaeologists believe the Serpent Mound was built by the same Adena Indians, and probably was used as a center for religious and burial rites.[14]

This site is situated in the northern part of Adams county, on the east bluff of Brush Creek, a short distance from the village of Locust Creek. With three burial mounds, it is included in a sixty acre area known as the Serpent Mound State Memorial.

In the State of Ohio, in fact, there are hundreds of prehistoric mounds, enclosures and cemeteries. And from the excavations made in the major sites, it is believed they were occupied (before Columbus) by at least five different groups of people known as *Fort Ancient, Erie, Cole, Hopewell,* and *Adena.*

Angel Mound, A.D. 1300-A.D. 1500, Middle Mississippian, east of Evansville, Indiana.

A Shawnee Indian Tradition
(Ohio River Valley)

"Cornstalk" (whose Indian name was *Keightughaua)* was the respected chief of the Shawnee Indians who lived in the Ohio River Valley in 1777. While visiting Captain William McKee, he said that "Ohio and Kentucky had once been settled by a white race possessed of arts of which the Indians had no knowledge, that after many sanguinary contests with the natives, these invaders were at length terminated." Cornstalk also told them that "the Great Spirit had once given the Indians a book which taught them all these arts; but they had lost it and had never since regained a knowledge of them."[15]

Fort Hill State Memorial
(Highland County, Ohio)

Located in Brush Creek Township, this site contains one of the best preserved prehistoric Indian hilltop enclosures in the state. Situated about four miles north of Sinking Springs, off of U.S. highway 50, it is one of the more scenic areas, containing interesting rock, plant and animal life, as well as foot trails leading to the ancient Hopewell Indian Earthworks.

Built by the Indians long before Columbus' arrival, it certainly exemplifies a major endeavor by a people who possessed only the simplest implements for digging and transporting the soil needed to create these earthworks and the enormous wall of earth and stone. Very few artifacts which might have helped to identify the builders were found. However, in one of the two circular earthworks south of Fort Hill, they found pottery fragments, flint spear points and other artifacts identified with the Hopewell Indians. The wall around the earthworks is one and five eighths miles in length with 33 openings or gateways.

The Hopewell Indians were renowned among the prehistoric cultures of the Upper Mississippi Valley, not only for their earthworks but also for their lovely ornaments and implements of stone, copper, shell, mica and bone. It is interesting to note they carried on extensive trade and commerce with other parts of the country—mica from the Carolinas, obsidian from the Rocky Mountains, copper from Michigan, ocean shells from the Gulf of Mexico and flint from even more distant sources.

There is every indication they had an elaborate social organization from which they drew, in order to plan and erect their rather sophisticated earthworks.

In 1838, John Locke (a geologist) wrote:

If. . .we add the probable period intervening from the time of the building of the work to its abandonment, and the subsequent period up to its invasion by the forest, we are led irresistibly to the conclusion that it has an antiquity of at least one thousand years. [16]

However, more modern carbon-14 tests indicate the Hopewell Indians lived in the Ohio Valley between 300 B.C. and A.D. 600. Therefore, Fort Hill is actually twice as old as archaeologists Squier and Davis had estimated. [17]

Angel Mounds State Memorial
(East of Evansville, Indiana)

This large prehistoric Indian town is 7 miles east on Indiana 662 to a point two and one-half miles west of Newburgh, down Fuquay Road to Pollack Avenue and 1/2 miles to the entrance. Here on the banks of the Ohio River a group who followed the *Mississippian* culture lived from A.D. 1300 to A.D. 1500. The settlement encompassed 103 acres, with a population of approximately 1,000 people. This important regional center has been under archaeological excavation for many years. Archaeologist Glenn A. Black believes these people were emigrants from Illinois, and possibly may not have been welcome, as they chose to build on a spot that was easy to defend. Inside the sturdy blockade which they built they erected eleven earth mounds, with three distinct terraces, many well-built residences and a plaza for community affairs. It appears that the Angel Site was a regional center which influenced the inhabitants of the small surrounding villages in the region.

Although this area was abandoned at the time of the first European contact, archaeologists have identified this group as *"Middle Mississippian."*

European explorers found the tribes of the Mississippi Valley living in well-ordered towns, building huge earthern mounds with imposing temples for worship of the sun. The Indians cultivated the rich bottom lands, hunted, fished, traded with their neighbors and even used pottery from distant places. This way of life spread over much of the Southeast, reached its peak around A.D. 1400 in this area, and began to decay by A.D. 1600. The name *Angel* was the family name of the people who once owned the mounds.[18]

Chucalissa Indian Town and Museum
(Chucalissa, Tennessee)

Traveling on U.S. 61 on the southern edge of Memphis, one may drive four and a half miles on Mitchell Road to the museum. The name Chucalissa is a word from modern Choctaw meaning "house abandoned."

This area was peopled around A.D. 900, and was thus continuously occupied for more than 700 years. It appears to be divided into two sections: (1) the ordinary people, and (2) the religious and political leaders.

The houses of the leaders—surrounding a plaza which fronted a temple—were made of poles or posts, finished with a mud and straw plaster, and a roof bearing overlapping bundles of long grass. The ceremonial temple which faced the plaza and the leaders' homes was constructed in the same way only much larger.

The treatment of this ancient temple indicates some strong parallels. At first the temple was built on a low foundation. Then, as years passed, one temple after another seemed to have been purposely burned, perhaps when a leader died or the group was conquered by invaders. Each building added height and width to the structure until finally a temple of considerable size dominated the area. This custom was evident in ancient Mexico, especially, and in particular the ruins of Cholula in southeastern Mexico. This structure represents at least seven or eight layers of architecture built by conquering groups who, with their victory, covered the old temple to indicate the end of that particular leadership.

Chucalissa Indian City and Museum, circa A.D. 900,
Chucalissa, near Memphis, Tennessee.

SOUTHEASTERN AREA

The Cherokee Indians

The Cherokee is the largest tribe in the Southeast, and fostered a religion traceable to a time before the white man came. Nevertheless, their teachings resembled much of what the European missionaries taught.

They believed that God could appear in the form of man, that He created the earth, and He knew all things and governed all things. Ancient tribal oral traditions speak of events very similar to the creation story, the confusion of tongues at a great tower, the twelve tribes of Israel and the crossing from the Old World by water.

There is always the question of whether these legends were influenced by early Christian missionaries, but their Meso-American and South American counterparts were also familiar with these stories. We can understand why Lord Kingsborough (Edward King) wrote the Aztecs of Mexico "...had a clear knowledge of the Old Testament, and most probably, of the New, though somewhat corrupted by time."[19]

In colonial times the Cherokee people tried to get along with their white neighbors, even taking their grievances to Washington instead of fighting. Yet no redress was obtained through this means, and the Indians were driven out of their own lands. The story of their persecution is called "The Trail of Tears," and stands as a black mark on the pages of American history, regarding the white man's treatment of the Indians.

Moundville
(near Tuscaloosa, Alabama)

This rich and impressive site, 17 miles south of Tuscaloosa (on Alabama 69), is now a National Historic Landmark because it is a combination of a museum as well as an archaeological site—the museum itself being constructed over two archaeological excavations. Its existence was not known to the public until 1848, when Squier and Davis reported it in *Ancient Monuments of the Mississippi Valley,* describing it as one of the largest mound groups in North America. Then, in 1905, Clarence B. Moore, a wealthy Philadelphian, made an expedition into this area and spent two months excavating the site. The enormous amounts of cultural material unearthed by Moore made Moundville one of the most spectacular sites in the western hemisphere. Because of this popularity, collectors and dealers began to vandalize and loot the area. Fortunately a group of caring local citizens banded together and were able to preserve this valuable prehistoric site for the enjoyment and education of future generations.

Moundville covers over 300 acres containing ancient living areas, 20 truncated (flat-top) earthern pyramids and a large central plaza. Some of the mounds range from 3 to 60 feet in height while others are from 12 to 15 feet high. There are also four lakes inside the wooden stockade. The Indians knew where to live. They obviously chose this site because of the rich soil which produced generous harvests of corn, squash, and other crops. It being a highland region, there was also considerable access to game animals such as deer and turkey.

It appears to be a peaceful, planned community, occupied from A.D. 1200 to A.D. 1400. An enormous burial site was discovered after over a decade of excavation by the Alabama Museum of Natural History, from 1929 through 1941. This effort resulted in the discovery of 3,000 burials, 75 dwelling sites, 100

Moundville, one of the largest in North America,
A.D. 1200 to A.D. 1400, Moundville, near Tuscaloosa, Alabama.

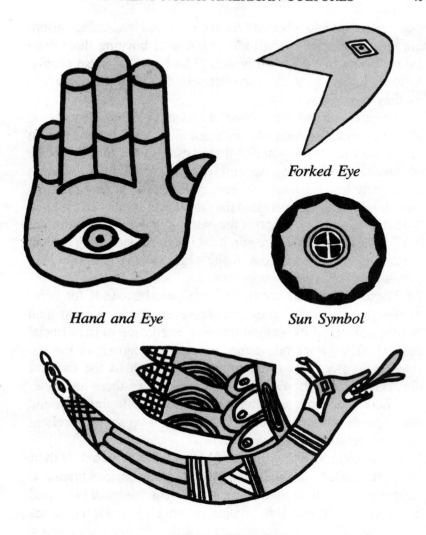

Forked Eye

Hand and Eye

Sun Symbol

Winged Serpent

Moundville symbols similar to those found in Teotihuacan, Mexico.

clay fire basins and other cultural material. An interesting custom among these people was their practice of burying their dead in the floors of their own homes. The bones of these prehistoric skeletons, as well as the items buried with them, remain as they were found.

The artifacts and items found at Moundville indicate its being a very peaceful community, with not only much hard work but also time for games—one of them being much like the game of lacrosse, involving several hundred men. The women apparently had the time and energy to create pottery that was quite lovely. They also created the Old World symbol of the hand with the All-seeing eye inside the palm. It is thought to represent the hand and eye of the Creator. This is a most interesting ancient custom. Even in Syria, today, many Arabs still use "eye-in-hand" decals on their vehicle windows.

These people did not build huge burial mounds for ceremonies and worship. They did, however, devote a great deal of time and effort to burying the dead according to their burial customs, always including the precious belongings of the deceased. It was from these graves that much of the cultural material was found, revealing many facets of their life-style.

There is an excellent museum in Moundville, built around two mounds which have been kept intact. Two short, excellent slide presentations are available.

In the history of the people of Moundville, a branch of their ancestors, called Tookabalchas, brought some curious brass and copper plates with them to Tuscaloosa—two plates of brass and five of copper. These were brought out once a year for the "brass plates dance." In dimensions, one of the copper plates was a foot-and-a-half long, and seven inches wide; the other four plates were a little shorter and narrower.

The shape of these two brass plates was circular, being about eighteen inches in diameter, with inscriptions on the plate. A reporter wrote that the Tookabalcha tribe had many more of these relics of varying sizes and shapes, with letters and inscriptions on them, which they claimed were given to them by the Great Spirit. Sometimes they would paint their bodies with colors and then inscribe themselves with hieroglyphs and representations of the sun, moon and stars.[20]

The author's first thoughts, upon entering the area and viewing the mounds row upon row, with the massive (restored) temple and steps leading to the top, were how reminiscent this was of the temples of Teotihuacan and Chichen Itza, in Mexico. In fact, the symbolic art of Moundville is indeed strikingly similar to the religious art of the same period in Mexico and Central America. Among the designs represented in Moundville Indian symbolism are the cross, the skull and crossbone, the weeping eye, the horned and plumed serpent, severed trophy heads, the hand and eye, and the dancing warrior.

Skull deformation was also practiced, with infants being placed on a cradle board with the head bound to the board with strips of soft hide. A pad was also placed on the forehead to flatten the front of the skull. This practice may have been an insignia of rank or status or even a mark of beauty.[21]

Moundville seems to be one of the more peaceful and culturally progressive civilizations, leaving much for us to study and appreciate.

Ocmulgee National Monument, occupied from circa 4000 B.C. to A.D. 1540, Macon, Georgia

Ocmulgee National Monument
(Macon, Georgia)

On the southeast edge of Macon, traveling on U.S. 80 East, we find one of the oldest and largest North American mounds called Ocmulgee (oak-MULL-gee) National Monument—*Ocmulgee* means "bubbling stream." This area was inhabited by several groups, or tribes, with the contemporary Indians knowing little or nothing of their ancestors and the origin of these mounds. One writer compared the human history in the Old and the New World as follows:

> In the Old World, human history has been traced to its beginnings through fossil remains suggesting a stage of development earlier than man. In the Western hemisphere, however, no such remains have been found, which indicates that the American Indian must have immigrated here from another continent. In searching for his closest relative, therefore, scientists are now agreed that certain physical peculiarities show the modern as well as the prehistoric Indian to be most closely linked to the peoples of eastern Asia.[22]

Six groups are believed to have lived in Ocmulgee during the periods indicated:

1. Paleo-Indian (9000-8000 B.C.)
2. Archaic (7000 B.C.)
3. Woodland (1000-500 B.C.)
4. Macon-Plateau (A.D. 900)
5. Resurgence (A.D. 1100)
6. Creek (A.D. 1540)

It wasn't until 1933 through 1941 that archaeological excavations established the importance and significance of Ocmulgee. The Master Farmers followed the hunters about A.D. 900, and began building elaborate villages with some very novel features. Being farmers, they were able to remain in one place for a longer period and thus develop a permanent religious and ceremonial city.

Ocmulgee includes a very large, flat-topped mound with a stairway ramp leading to the top where a sacred temple once stood. Other surrounding hills were both burial mounds and areas of worship 200 years ago. The refuse mounds are measured by *stratigraphy,* and are about 5,000 years old. The science of studying ancient garbage dumps has provided archaeologists with a great deal of information on America's prehistory.

During their prehistoric occupancy, temple stuctures also existed atop these mounds. The large mound with a stairway was believed to be the one used for summer harvest ceremonies. The custom of succeeding generations covering and changing these temple mounds links them with areas such as Cholula, Mexico, where seven enormous sturctures were built, one over the other, by conquering groups. The steps leading up to the worship center at Ocmulgee reminded the author of similar ancient temples in Central America.

The excellent museum at Ocmulgee tells this story, and much more, through models, dioramas of family life anciently, artifacts and potters—some of it quite beautiful.

Bynum Mounds
(near Tupelo, Mississippi)

Not far from Chucalissa and near Tupelo, one can travel southwest on the Natchez Trace Parkway and, following the markers, visit the Bynum Mounds. No trucks are permitted on this beautiful highway dedicated to local historical sites commemorating historical events. Indians dwelt in the woods along this roadway, and markers even indicate that "DeSoto traveled this way."

The Bynum Mounds are not flashy, but they are different—representing the settlement of a Woodland Indian tribe who lived here anciently. They buried their dead in special places with pots and personal items surrounding the bodies. Six of these mounds were found near the village. According to the artifacts found nearby (now in the Information Center at Tupelo), these people did a great deal of trading with Indians as far away as Lake Superior. They built circular houses thatched with grass, hunted, fished, gathered wild fruits and nuts, and even maintained small gardens. As time passed they began building earthen mounds over their dead, which was a custom of the times.

Shiloh Military National Park
(Tennessee)

This park is about 10 miles south of Savannah and Adamsville, Tennessee, traveling four miles west on U.S. 64 and six miles south on Tennessee 22.

There are more than 30 mounds in this park. Two types of mounds overlooking a beautiful river were built by pre-Spanish Indians. The earlier dome-shaped earthwork covered their burials, and the later flat-topped mounds were used as ceremonial temples. It is interesting to note that local scholars have decided the temples built upon other temples were erected in honor of a new chief, which the author has explained previously. This indicates a possible strong connection with the Indians to the south, in Mexico and Central and South America. And, this was not solely a custom with the prehistoric Indians. Anciently the Greeks followed a similar custom of destruction: the statues of ancient fallen leaders with their heads cut off are a common sight to the visitor today when visiting Greece. The ancient Americans, not being one to create much statuary, translated this custom into destroying or covering existing temples.

PLAINS AREA

Indian City
(Anadarko, Oklahoma)

This fascinating village represents a unique example of development for the enjoyment and education of travelers in the United States. Designed as a vast outdoor museum, Indian City offers the highly accurate reproduction of American Indian villages in a beautiful and natural setting. It is the cultural center for several tribes originating in this area.

Certainly, Oklahoma's history is firmly bound to historic and prehistoric Indian life and art. Due to the cooperation between the state of Oklahoma and the Commission of Oklahoma Indian Affairs, an upsurge of pride amongst the Indian people has taken place. All buildings were constructed under the supervision of the Department of Anthropology of the University of Oklahoma.

Oklahoma is considered to be the melting pot of Indian America. Even the name *Oklahoma* comes from the Choctaw Indian words, "Okla," meaning *people,* and "humma" or "homma" meaning *red,* thus literally meaning *Red People.*

When the author visited Indian City, Alton Stumblingbear, the guide, explained that he was a descendant of a long line of chiefs, from both his mother and father. His royal lineage came through the Kiowa and Plain Apache Indians.

In the village, tepees are set up as they once were, in circles, with a recreation and work pavilion for each area. Originally, most had a circle of tepees, a shaded work and recreation area, a rack for drying meat, and a council room.

Each tepee in the Paconee Village had an altar for worship. Included in their Indian traditions is a belief in the Creator—one God whom they call "Big Brother"—and also an oral tradition concerning the creation of the world. Pipe smoking is considered a ceremonial communication with their Creator, repeated each day as the sun rises. The smoke is thought to curl upward from the pipe to the Creator.

In a Paconee home, two to three families shared a tepee, with a cookfire in the center and bamboo, reed-supported beds covered with fur, on the side. A calendar written on skins indicated family and tribal activities for the year. A butterfly found in a corner of the calendar symbolized eternal life.

The tepee (also spelled *tipi*) was the traveling home of the Kiowa, Comanche, Arapaho, and other roaming Plains Indian tribes. In Indian City, one views a typical winter camp with two large tepees set up near a windbreaker—a fence of willow branches and grass surrounding the camp.

This 160-acre tract of land is rich in history—a small portion of the once-huge Kiowa, Comanche and Apache reservation. The Tokawa Massacre (by a band of Shawnees and some mercenaries) also took place on the hills of Indian City during the Civil War.

The Indian master farmers had a special funeral mound on the western edge of the town of Indian City, Oklahoma, containing graves and once boasting a temple. These mounds contained the bones of tribal chiefs and leaders wrapped in bundles and laid out in a natural position in log tombs or simple graves. Tools, weapons, food and ornaments were placed in the grave for use by the dead in their afterlife. This, of course, is very similar to burial traditions in ancient Peru, where weapons, tools and food were placed within the burial mound for the deceased to use in their afterlife.

Another of the seven villages at Indian City is the home of
a nomadic hunting tribe which struggled for a meager existence
in the deserts of the Southwest. Other villages were inhabited
by buffalo-hunting tribes such as the well-known Plains Indians.

Indian City, USA, is a corporation organized by the citizens
of Anadarko, many of whom have seen the transition from the
Indian way to the white man's civilization. It is a living memorial
to the American Indian. One reason for the organization of
Indian City was to provide opportunities for the Indians to work,
make and sell their arts and crafts. It is also a place where the
Indian and the white man can meet and exchange ideas.

Of additional interest in the various villages are the numerous
artifacts on display in the reconstructed dwellings. Items such
as tools, cradles, cooking utensils, weapons, musical instruments, games and toys of the various tribes exhibited in their
original manner.

The most impressive of all the villages at Indian City is that
of the Wichita, principally because of its 40-foot-high Council
House. The fact that the women did all the building in the
Wichita tribe makes the structure all the more interesting and
impressive. Pine poles split in half were set in the ground in
a circle and joined together at the top. This framework was then
covered with willow branches and swamp grass to provide a
completely weatherproof dwelling. In addition to the Council
House, the Wichita village includes a community shelter where
women gathered to do their work. In this structure are various
racks for drying meat, vegetables and buffalo skins.

These were the real Plains Indians. As far back as history
records, Indians from Kansas to Texas lived in a particular way.
Farms were individually owned, not like the communal practice
of the Caddo tribe. The women did the work, while the men
hunted for game. Buffalo was an extremely valuable source of
meat, fur, and skins for bedding and clothing.

The Caddo Indians from Texas and Louisiana were farmers and hunters. Caddo women planted and gardened, while the men took care of the hunting. They built more permanent homes than the roaming tribes, leading quiet, peaceful lives. Wood, which was plentiful, was used in the homes for heating and cooking. The Caddos now live primarily in the area north of Anadarko, Oklahoma.

Although the Pawnee Indians were once part of the Caddoan tribe, they built a different type of dwelling and house of worship. Their homes were permanent and built to withstand the cold winter as well as the heat of the summer. The people were deeply religious and each home contained an alter for worship ceremonies. Because they were peaceful in nature, the pawnees were often in demand as U.S. Army guides and scouts.

Representing the Pawnee way of life are two "earth lodges" at Indian City. Upon first examination, the lodges appear to be simple humpback dugouts or man-made caves. Inside, however, the visitor is surprised to see that they are much more elaborate structures: large poles mark off the center area, which was the domain of the wife—her kitchen. At the far end of the lodge, opposite the entrance, is the family altar (the domain of the head man or elder of the household). Around the outer wall of the remainder of the dwelling is a two-foot high ledge covered with willow branches, buffalo hides, and furs used for sitting and sleeping.

As the author viewed the Indian villages, he was reminded of the time when the various tribes lived throughout the Americas in their organized villages, before the United States government placed them on reservations. Theirs was even a sacred tribal leadership. The white man has never understood the reverence Indians have felt in their relationship to God's great earth, which they have been allowed to use—never taking any more from it than was needful.

What the white man might consider "lack of progress" is, in a sense, the Indian concept of man and the earth, working with the Creator in the delicate cycle of life and survival.

Indian City, 40' council house, Wichita, Anadarko, Oklahoma.

Indian City, Caddo house, Anadarko, Oklahoma.

Indian City, "Travois," transportation vehicle, Anadarko, Oklahoma.

Indian City, Indian burial, Anadarko, Oklahoma.

*Indian City, stretched, dried buffalo hide,
Anadarko, Oklahoma.*

Indian City, framework for a teepee, Anadarko, Oklahoma.

Indian City, a Pawnee kitchen, with bedroom in background, Anadarko, Oklahoma.

Indian City, bones—animals of prey, Anadarko, Oklahoma.

Mammoth Hot Springs Visitors' Center
(Yellowstone National Park)

Traveling from the north entrance to the park on U.S. 89, one can drive to the Visitors' Center. Of the five exhibits on display, one concentrates on prehistoric art work and Indian relics found in the park.

Pictograph Cave
(Between Billings and Hardin, Montana)

Northward from Yellowstone, and seven miles off U.S. 87, between Billings and Hardin, Montana, is a large pictograph cave, believed to have been inhabited as early as 3000 B.C.

Early photographs on display are better than an actual visit to the caves, since most of the drawings have been destroyed by vandals. This is a tragedy.

Mandan Slant Indian Village
(Mandan, North Dakota)

Traveling about four and a half miles south of Mandan, on North Dakota 6, is the restored Mandan Slant Indian Village—named thusly because of the sloping ground on which it was situated. Five of the dwellings have been restored and appear much like the circular earth lodges of late prehistoric times. Scholars believe it to be the most important site of all the Mandan ruins in North Dakota. This group presumably moved from the south to this location sometime in the 1600s.

The dome-shaped circular homes were 30 to 40 feet in diameter and about 10 feet high. Inside, the beds were along the left wall, with the right wall containing a stall for horses. In the center was a fireplace dug into the ground, with a ventilation hole directly above. Skins covered this "chimney" during severe weather. All lodges faced the center of the village. In an open area is a ring of poles called "the ark of the first man," a religious memorial commemorating the Mandan legend

Slant Village, "Ring of Poles," A.D. 1600, Fort Lincoln State Park, Mandan, North Dakota.

of a wise man in their tribe who built a similar structure, hurried the tribal members into it and saved them from drowning in an enormous flood which covered the world.[23]

On the subject of the flood legend amongst the Indians, the author has in his possession a small and valuable book published by Albert B. Reagan, Ph. D., a professor of anthropology, who served as an official in the United States Indian Field Service from 1899 to 1934. It was from this experience that he documented the legend of the flood among 23 Indian groups in North and Central America.[24] Historians generally agree that the story of the "Ark," with its religious connotations, was an ancient Indian tradition in many tribes.

Sherman Park
(Sioux Falls, South Dakota)

In the Sherman Park at Sioux Falls, South Dakota, are several mounds built by a prehistoric people who followed the Woodland lifeway about 1600 years ago. These mounds were excavated in 1973 by W.H. Over. Bones of the dead and burial artifacts were found.

Sherman Park Mounds, circa A.D. 400, Plains-Woodland, Sioux Falls, South Dakota.

Koster Site
(50 Miles north of St. Louis, Missouri;
270 miles southwest of Chicago).

The traveler may visit this fascinating site by driving from Eldred on Illinois 108, then proceeding five and a half miles south on the Grafton blacktop road.

For years Theodore Koster unearthed potsherds every time he plowed his field near the Illinois River. Therefore, in 1969, his neighbor Harlin Helton persuaded Dr. Stuart Streuver, of Northwestern University, to investigate the findings on Mr. Koster's farm. The subsequent digging astonished and delighted the archaeological crew. By 1973, excavation had revealed that for possibly 6,000 years 15 different groups had made their home here at the foot of a limestone bluff. Each time a group left, the debris was gradually covered by each washing down from the bluff, gradually becoming what Dr. Streuver called a "fossilized layer cake—soft soil, then the debris; another sterile layer of silt and another treasure of archaeological remains, and so on through fifteen levels and 34 feet of ancient so-called horizons." Dr. Streuver was also of the opionion that even older layers of habitation might lay beneath the 15th level. Other excavations have uncovered multiple "horizons," but the Koster site is the first where archaeologists have found such extensive prehistoric village areas, one above the other, so clearly defined and easily dated. Men from nearly a dozen areas of scientific discipline joined to piece together the fascinating story of early man in Illinois. They came up with some surprising findings:

1. A palynologist (pollen specialist) identified corn pollen on Horizon 6, dated at 2500 B.C.—indicating that corn was cultivated in Illinois two thousand years or more before such a thing was believed to be likely.

Koster Site, circa 2500 B.C. onward, occupied by 15 groups, 50 miles north of St. Louis, Missouri, 270 miles southwest of Chicago, Illinois.

2 . An expert on animal bones found another surprise:
the skeletal remains of a domestic dog at least five
thousand years old.

The Koster Site scientists felt they were in a position to
dispute some long-held archaeological theories concerning early
man living chiefly from the hunt, but also depended upon plant
food for survival.

The excavation not only provided some answers, but also
raised some questions, such as:

1 . why was this such a favorable site for such a long
period, then abandoned for long periods of time?

2 . why did the population increase so slowly, with all
the abundant resources? and

3 . why, at one level, did most of the burials yield the
skeletal remains of so many young people?

Scientists at the Koster site are using modern and sophisticated procedures linked to a computer in order to try to find
the answers. It is a major prehistoric Indian site. The work being
done here makes it an exciting place.

The work continues. Who knows what new treasures will
be unearthed at this and other ancient American sites? Certainly
scientists do not have all the answers, with their guidelines
constantly changing. Much truth still lies hidden in the earth.

Dickson Mounds Museum
(Between Lewiston and Havana, Illinois)

If travelers drive three miles from Lewiston on U.S. 24, then two miles south on Illinois 78 to a directional sign, they will come to a fascinating Illinois State Museum known as Dickson Mounds. A new building has been erected which is a replica of a prehistoric mound found here—representing the Archaic, Woodland, and Mississippian cultural periods (comprising the prehistory of what is now the eastern half of the United States). Built in 1972, it is one of the few on-site museums. A multimedia approach is used for many of the presentations in the excellent museum.

This site was discovered in 1927, by Dr. Don F. Dickson, a physician, who launched his own scientific investigation of the human bones found on his land. Finally, what had begun as a medical study regarding disease in prehistoric times turned into a full-fledged archaeological excavation, providing much information regarding prehistoric Indians. There is so much to be learned from this area which the state has financed for ongoing research at the site—over 1,000 mounds and villages sites are known, in Fulton County alone.[25]

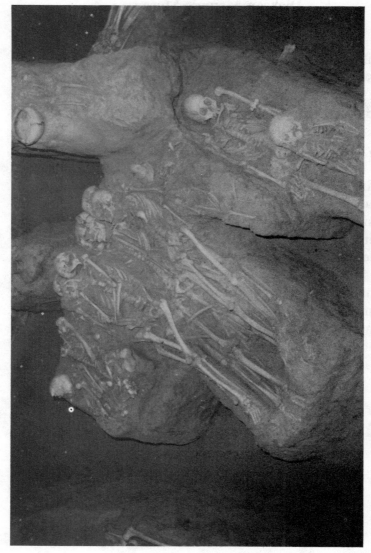

Dickson Mounds Museum, Indian burial site, Fulton County, near Lewiston and Havana, Illinois.

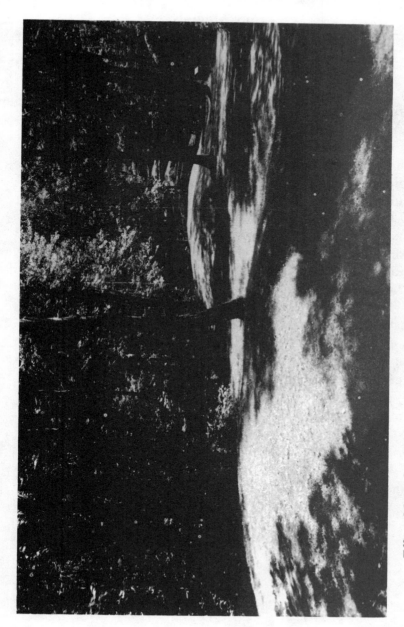

Effigy Mounds, 1500 years of continuous existence, near Marquette, Iowa.

Effigy Mounds
(Near Marquette, Iowa)

A visitor can travel three miles north of Marquette, on Iowa 76, and visit the Effigy Mounds, built on high ground next to the Mississippi River. The Indians built nearly 200 mounds during a period of 1500 years, some of which are likenesses (effigies) of animals; others are cone shaped.

The earliest tools discovered near these mounds are wood-working implements—axes, adzes, gauges. Other evidence indicates the people hunted forest animals, fished and gathered wild rice, nuts, fruits and berries.

They developed unique burial practices, often painting the bones of the dead with red ocher after allowing the body to disintegrate. Many divergent customs were introduced into this area through more than 1500 years of continuous existence by various groups.

The first mention of Effigy Mound was made in approximately 1768 in a book by Jonathan Carver, *Travels Through the Interior Parts of North America in the Years 1766, 1767, 1768.* But it was in 1881 that Theodore H. Lewis and Alfred J. Hill began an intensive study of the mound groups of the Mississippi River, resulting in excellent maps of the mounds throughout the southern United States. In 1949 Effigy Mounds went into Federal ownership—over 1200 acres and 99 mounds being perserved for our education and enjoyment today.

It is also an extremely scenic area, in which travelers may enjoy magnificent panoramic views of the Mississippi River, as well as *guided* and *self-guided* tours through marked trails to see the flora and fauna as well as the mounds.

Monk's Mound or Cahokia Mounds at State Park
(Cakokia, Illinois, five miles east of St. Louis, Missouri)

The author reached this magnificent site by traveling from St. Louis, Missouri, eastward five miles on Interstate 55-70 to Route 111 exit, then southward to U.S. 40 (Collinsville Rd); then going left one-and-a-half miles to the park entrance. This famous mound contains 650 acres and is believed to be the largest archaeological site in North America—a man-made pyramid of earth 100 feet high and surrounded by 40 smaller mounds. It is in reality a true pyramid or temple, measuring 1,000 feet at the base, north to south, and 100 feet high. At one time, it boasted a population of thirty to forty thousand Woodland people—a population more dense than at any other place in America north of the Valley of Mexico. This statistic alone reflects the prosperity and vigor which made Cahokia an influential center from which the Mississippian culture spread throughout the surrounding lands.

The idea of placing their public buildings on earthen mounds to elevate them above their town probably came from Mexico. The large open plazas in front of these pyramids also gave them great distinction. They had great success with their crops on the rich land of Cahokia, and as time passed the number of mounds increased. The Woodland people prospered through trading, shipping their goods on the nearby Mississippi River. The number of mounds within the 4,000-acre region grew to about 120, until growth suddenly ceased about A.D. 1500, when the site was abandoned. At the present time approximately 130 mounds have been uncovered.

Evidence indicates the Cahokians sought good harvests by conducting ceremonies which included sacrifice of their most valuable possessions, including human life. This practice also existed in Mexico. Some scholars and scientists are of the opinion that the Cahokian culture could have originated from the south, migrating northward up the Mississippi River.

Cahokia Mounds or Monk's Mound, at its cultural zenith, one of the largest archaeological sites in North America, Cahokie, Illinois, 5 miles east of St. Louis, Missouri. (Artist's rendering, courtesy of Richard Schlecht, National Geographic [December, 1972], pp. 788-89.)

A portion of the remains of Cahokia or Monk's Mound complex, Woodland, to A.D. 1500, one of the largest prehistoric cities in North America.

A man-made mound indicates a great deal about a civilization. It possesses a definite shape. It is a planned community, and therefore more permanent. Mound building indicates a division of labor—with planners or leaders, and those who carried out the work—the rulers and the ruled. In other words, it was an indication of social classes. There was a social strata here, possibly consisting of leaders, agriculturalists, and mound builders.

These earthen pyramids also indicated a strong religious belief in immortality, judging from the manner in which they buried their dead—often amid riches and nearly always under massive heaps of earth. They attempted to create circumstances which might lie ahead for their honored dead, surrounding them with blankets, clothing, food, weapons, tools and amulets—a testimony of their belief in the reality of an afterlife. These moundbuilders not only lived within the sacred realm of nature, but also elaborated life in a more sophisticated manner than previous cultures.

Named after the trappist monks who once farmed on top of the temple mound (Monk's Mound), Cahokia Mounds State Park is possibly the most spectacular ancient site in North America. Because it is almost as big as the pyramid of Cheops in Egypt, the author has included an artist's concept of this earthen pyramid and city at its cultural zenith.

Lyman Archaeological Research Center, Utz Indian Village
(Four miles west of Marshall, Missouri)

Located in Van Meter State Park, this archaeological center and school has been erected on the site of a large prehistoric Indian village known as the *Utz Site*. Scientific excavations take place each summer from June through August. Artifacts from this dig reveal items from the Archaic, Hopewell, Woodland and Oneota cultures, and are on display in the museum nearby.

Salina Burial Museum
(Four miles from Salina, Kansas)

This museum is built over a cemetery protecting 146 ancient burials. Unearthed by archaeologists, they were found with knees drawn up and hands resting close to their faces. Some of the skeletons are quite large, measuring well over six feet in height. Present research has not yet established a date for this civilization.

The ancient practice of burying the dead in an embryonic position is also found in Peru. The bodies were also wrapped with blankets, surrounded by food, tools and valuable items, as found in the burials at Cahokia Mounds. This is a small but interesting museum.

Utz Indian Village, Lyman Archaeological Research Center, Van Meter State Park, near Marshall, Missouri.

Salina burial Museum, built over a prehistoric cemetery. Salina, Kansas.

SOUTHWESTERN INDIANS AREA

In the geographic area of Arizona, New Mexico, California, Nevada and Utah, 170,000 Indians now live on reservations. The Navajos, the most populous tribe in the United States, live on 16 million acres in northeast Arizona, northwest New Mexico, and southern Utah. The Southwestern Indian area covers Arizona, New Mexico, southern Utah and Colorado. There are nineteen separate Pueblo groups in New Mexico, from which come the Hopi people who live on an "island" in the middle of the Navajo reservation. Other groups with Pueblo roots are Acoma, Laguna, San Iidefonso, Taos, Zia, and Zuni. Apaches live on reservations in both New Mexico and Arizona; Ute and Paiute live in Utah, Colorado, and northern New Mexico; and other tribes of the area include Papago, Pima, Chemehuevi, Cocopah, Mojave, Havasupai, Hualapai, Havapi, Maricopa, Waiguri, Yaqui and Yuma. More Indians live in Arizona than in any other state in the nation—100,000 people from fourteen different tribes, with 19 reservations covering 27% of the state's land.

Rich in archaeological relics, it invites the scholar and the scientist to examine their surprisingly advanced civilizations which existed here thousands of years ago.

The Pueblo Indians are one of the oldest groups in the Southwestern area. In fact, the ancestors of today's Pueblo Indians refer to their ancient cultures with a Hopi word, *Anasazi*, which means "the ancient ones." They were considered a peaceful people who fought only when attacked. They were excellent craftsmen and built the great cliff houses which were virtually abandoned by the end of the thirteenth century. It was the Spanish who called them "Pueblos," which means "villages" in their language. It has been learned that even the people in the Pueblos group were not tribally related, as each pueblo was established as an indepedent society. The Anasazi found their way into many areas of the Southwestern region, and became the roots of numerous modern tribal groups.

The Papago and Pima Indians of southern Arizona are believed by many archaeologists to be descendants of a culture even older than the Azasazi. They are called *Hohokam*—a Pima word meaning, "those who have vanished." Their achievements include extensive irrigation systems which were well developed by A.D. 700.[26]

Navajo Indians

Famous today for elegant woolen blankets, fine silver and turquoise jewelry and an intriguing way of life, the Navajo tribe, at this point in time, is growing faster than any other American minority group. Navajo is a Spanish word, but the approximately 120,000 Indians (compared to 16,000 a century ago) call themselves *Deneh* (pronounced Dih-nay), which means "The People." Proud and dignified, they are more solemn and shy in their contacts with the white people—more than any other tribe.

Little is known of the early Navajo history, only that sometime between A.D. 1000 and 1500 their Athabascan ancestors migrated into the Southwest in small groups from the North. They were known as fierce warriors. During the Spanish and Mexican rule they were never conquered. And even during the first twenty years of U.S. jurisdiction they remained unconquered. Only when they were starved into surrender, in 1864, did they finally capitulate to Colonel Kit Carson. This represents the epic of the "long walk," from the beautiful area of Canyon de Chelly (pronounced "de-shay") when eight thousand Navajos—half the tribe—traveled to Fort Sumner, New Mexico, and were confined for four years. Many Navajos died on this march. Then, in the Treaty of 1868, they were allowed to return to a portion of their homeland—another tragic chapter in the annals of Indian-U.S. relationships.

One may visit this fascinating area by traveling north from State 264 about six miles west of Ganado. After thirty miles take the right fork, drive through Chinle, Arizona, and continue to the Canyon de Chelly National Monument headquarters.

The Navajo reservation is geographically the largest in the United States; as large as Massachusetts, New Hampshire and Vermont combined. Even though it is an arid, badly eroded land, it is a majestically scenic and wild area, ranging from high mountains to deep canyons, with famous natural bridges. Some of the land is well suited for grazing of sheep, which is the Navajo's principal occupation, but water is scarce and irrigation limited—however, much land could be productive if irrigation were possible. Mutton, beans, and fried bread are the mainstays of the Navajo diet. Their famous Indian taco is a delicious meal—one the author recommends, if you ever see it advertised in any restaurant in Navajoland.

The sale of sheep and wool provides the bulk of their income, which is approximately $2,000 per year. Their beautifully woven and intricately designed hand-loomed wool rugs are in demand throughout the world and command a high price. Next in importance to Navajo industry is lumbering and mining, followed by agriculture in areas where water is plentiful. The San Juan Basin produces great quantities of petroleum and natural gas, with the proceeds from the leases going to the tribal treasury. With the discovery of oil and minerals on their reservation, the Navajo Tribal Council was organized to negotiate and sign these agreements. This has helped to improve their economy, which has brought about improved housing, recreation, health and education facilities, self-help and self-respect.

Home to a Navajo is his hogan (pronounced *ho-gahn*)—a roughly circular log and adobe structure with a domed roof.

The door always faces east, and there may or may not be a window. This dwelling is cool in summer and warm in winter. Sheepskins and rugs are used as bedding. In earlier times, hogans were built with three heavy poles like a tripod, but later the hexagonal shape became more popular. They are made of logs much like a log cabin, except the roof is conical, drawing inward toward a smoke hole for cooking and heat.

Many Navajo families now live in wooden frame houses or adobe buildings, but the hogan remains. They are widely scattered and isolated, with the customary village clusters almost nonexistent. One can see the hogans and other structures today when traveling through the southwest. In the proper season the traveler may also visit the roadside shops where beautiful silver and turquoise jewelry and other arts and crafts are handcrafted for sale to the public.

The author has included photographs taken of the two modes of structure used by the Navajos today and in earlier times. The earlier hogan was constructed of pine logs laid horizontally in a circular criss-cross, in such a way as to resemble the shape of a beehive, and covered with a mixture of adobe clay. The other hogan is a more modern structure—one still in use by the Navajos. In these circular homes, pine timbers are first set in the ground horizontally and in a circle. The walls are then constructed of pine logs set vertically, with the conical roof then built onto this, as in the original hogan. An outdoor oven for baking bread is also pictured—still a very functional part of the Navajo community.

Weaving, like farming learned from their Pueblo Indian neighbors, has become associated with the Navajo almost more than any other tribe. The Navajo blanket is a treasured possession that will, with care, last a lifetime. Weaving is considered a woman's work. She washes the wool, prepares it, dyes some of the yarn and does the weaving. The design is in their heads,

Navajo hogan, late model.

Navajo hogan, early beehive construction.

Young Navajo girl, Navajo Indian Reservation.
Monument Valley, Arizona.

Monument Valley, (northern) Arizona.

passed down from one generation to another. The meaning is known only to the weaver, and no design is ever repeated exactly. However, general patterns also are used, and some dyes account for the brilliant colors interspersed with natural black, white, grey and brown wool.

Sand painting is also an art in which the Navajo man is supreme. Clean sand is spread over the floor of a space on which pictures are created with red, yellow, and black dry sands sifted between the thumb and finger. These works of art have a unique style all their own.

It has always been a source of amazement to the author, in his travels throughout the world, to observe how people living in the harshest of settings can examine the natural world around them and create their own matchless art and beauty from the most simple elements of the earth.

Anasazi

Long before the arrival of the ancient Athabascans from the north, the Pueblo-dwelling Indians of New Mexico had established their culture in the Southwest. Known as "the ancient ones," the Hopi and Pueblo Indians are among the proud descendants of the Anasazi group. These rugged people built great prehistoric cities such as the Cliff Dwellings in Mesa Verde National Park, which accommodated thousands. No one knows why they were abandoned by the thirteenth century. Others lived in Pit houses—partially underground.

The anasazi culture is found throughout the Southwest and Great Basin areas. Today they are called "the basket makers," even using them sometimes to cook their food—taking hot stones from the fire and placing them in the basket of food.

They also made hair combs from bones and feathers—also using bones, stones, shells and feathers to make jewelry. They ground their corn on stone metates, as did the Meso-Americana groups. They also ate the meat their men found through hunting, as well as beans, squash, nuts, berries and greens. Later the Anasazi also made pottery, enabling them to cook on their fires.[27]

An oustanding ancient site has been found in an area called Anasazi Valley, eight miles west and north of St. George, Utah (just two hours east of Las Vegas). An archaeological team has charted four ancient Indian dwellings in an 80-acre area—one civilization even atop another, which makes the site very old and possibly dates back to the time of Christ. There are also petroglyphs in the surrounding hills. The owner, Shela D. Wilson, plans to make the area into an Indian Cultural Center to protect and preserve the Indian dwellings for the public to enjoy. Other plans include shops for Indian groups from all the Americas to make and sell their beautiful rugs, jewelry, pottery, clothing and art. An extensive museum and amphitheatre for the performing arts are also planned, in addition to a wooded area by the river where authentic Indian dwellings will be erected.

Mesa Verde Ruins, near Cortez, Colorado.

Mesa Verde, Colorado

If one travels on U.S. 160, midway between Cortez and Mancos, he can turn south at the park entrance and drive 21 miles on the park road to the Museum and park headquarters.

Mesa Verde (pronounced *May-suh Ver-day)* is actually an enormous outdoor archaeological museum with many different sites, occupying a stretch of high flat land which looks like a huge table—hence the name "mesa," which in Spanish means "table." This mesa is surrounded by deep canyons and steep cliff walls. In these cliffs the prehistoric people sought their shelter in caves and rocks, eventually building some of the most beautiful and interesting pre-Columbian "apartments" or villages found in the southwest.

Mesa Verde was one of three areas where the Anasazi reached an extremely high point of culture before A.D. 1276—the others being Chaco Canyon and Kayenta. These people lived here for about 800 years and then mysteriously abandoned the cliff dwellings by 1276.

The traveler will gain a more complete picture of this culture, in each of its stages, by first visiting the museum in the Park Headquarters. The excellent displays and scaled models of this site help us understand their prehistoric life; the basketmakers, viewing the pottery, the bows and arrows, the use of fiber, plants and hair to weave cords; the pit houses, the stone houses, then the caves in the cliffs. These apartment-like dwellings were all built within the crescent-shaped hollows of the cliffs. Entrance to these cliff houses was usually by ladder, thus combining the privacy of a home with the protection of a fortress. For about a hundred years they lived atop the mesas and tossed their garbage over the cliffs, which resulted in great treasures for archaeological study.

The Sun temple at Mesa Verde is probably visited more often by the people of the United States than any other Indian site.

The ruin atop the mesa overlooking Cliff Palace Canyon is in an excellent state of preservation. Scholars belive it was erected by the Bow Clan for special ceremonies, with the immense structure facing east, following the design of a bow with a drawstring. The northern half of the building consists of one row of thirteen rooms surrounding an open plaza, within which are two kivas.

Hopi Indians

The name *Hopi* means "peaceful and righteous," and they are and have always been known as the people who seek peace. Several interesting traditions are found among the Hopis. In a personal interview in a Hopi community in the summer of 1978, the author learned that their beliefs include such tenets as baptism for the dead, eternal marriage, a strong religious priesthood, and that they are originally from Jerusalem, coming to Arizona from the south.

Although the Navajos far outnumber the Hopi, the latter claim to have arrived long before their more numerous neighbors. The Hopis are Shoshonean-speaking descendants of the ancient Anasazi city builders. As the Hopi developed their community life, each village had its own leader who was either elected or inherited the office.

The Hopis are agriculturalists. Their fields of corn, beans, squash and melons lie close to their villages and below their mesas. Only in a few places are their lands irrigated. Hopi women produce very good pottery—typically yellow, orange or reddish in a style used by their people in the fourteenth century. Their basketry is also in demand, as it is more colorful than those of the other Indian groups.

The Hopis live in twelve pueblo villages in a 600-square-mile area in the midst of the Navajo reservation in northeastern Arizona. No photographs are allowed within the older villages, due to supersition and religious reasons. Only the modern Hopi will permit the traveler to take their picture. One of these older villages is called Old Oraibi—said to be the oldest continuously inhabited settlement in the United States, having been established about A.D. 1150. Within these communities are family clans, each emphasizing a certain aspect of their culture through specific dances unique to their tribes. The approximately fifty clans combine to make a total population of seven thousand citizens.

The Hopis are deeply religious. Their concept of diety rests with the idea of a God who appoints a creator to work out the universes in proper order so that men may work harmoniously. Some of their medicine men have a small crystal which they believe will guide them in determining the cause of illness. The preparation of *pahos* is a prime requisite of all ceremonies conducted in the Kiva. A *paho* is a prayer-feather, usually taken from an eagle. Washing of the hair is also considered a sacred ceremony amongst the Hopi.

One of the most persistent Hopi legends concerns the return of their lost white brother, Pahana. Another important aspect of their religious faith is connected with four sacred tablets. One was given to the Fire clan and three to the Bear clan. One of the tablets has a missing corner. The legend presists that the one who provides the missing corner will be the one who will deliver them from their present predicament and set up a perfect brotherhood. The most detailed description of these tablets and their interpretation is provided by Frank Waters in his *Book of the Hopi*.[28] All the tablets, according to this tradition, are said to be yet in the possession of the Hopis—still very sacred. It is forbidden that they be shown to any white man.

The author and his university colleagues visited Old Oraibi, Arizona and were introduced to the leader who was supposed to have one of these tablets. However, he refused to show it to any of us.

The kiva is the Hopi structure wherein religious cermonies (exclusive of dances) are preformed. The kiva is symbolic of

Entrance to a Hopi Kiva used for religious ceremonies.

Reconstructed Hopi Kiva.

mother earth. A small hole in the middle of the floor represents the womb, and a ladder leading out through the roof represents the umbilical cord. This house of worship serves not only as a ceremonial center but also as a clubhouse for the men. Sometimes the women participate in the meetings in the kiva if they know the rituals. It is here the medicine men practice their cures, where initiated men don masks, feathered headdresses, and bizarre costumes—assuming the characters of the Kachinas duplicated in their dolls, which represent the members of the Hopi spirit world. The Hopi Kachina masked dancers represent the various spirits who accept petitions for *rain, health, and good fortune.* Small effigies of Kachina spirits are also given to the Hopi children.

The snake dance, a rain ceremony, usually occurs in late August. The Hopis, costumed in brightly decorated kilts and fox skins dance with live snakes. They believe the snakes will carry messages to the rain gods, informing them of the need for moisture.

The author feels there may be an Oriental connection to the Hopi culture. He once engaged a Chinese secretary born in Hong Kong. One day, as she was crossing the campus, a Hopi Indian stopped her and asked, "Are you Hopi?" We discussed how very much Ivy would resemble the Hopis in her appearance if she put on their traditional clothing. In Edmund Nequatewa's book, *Truth of a Hopi,* editor Mary-Russell F. Colton comments on this subject:

> Hopi philosophy has an oriental suggestion. The Hopi is, in many of his beliefs, a fatalist and believes that he and his clan are predestined to do certain things. This idea, or philosophy of life, he calls his "theory". . . handed down to a leading man by his uncles or great uncles on the maternal side, and there is also one clan woman who tells her grandsons of this "theory."[29]

Modern Pueblo

The modern-day Pueblo Indians are descendants of the prehistoric Anasazi tribe. Over 1,500 years ago, the Pueblo culture was in its early stages of development, breaking off from nomadic groups to enter into a semi-agricultural existence. Their fine basketry led archaeologists to give them the name *Basketmakers*.

There are three major language groups among the New Mexico Pueblos, and even further divisions in dialects within these three. Each village is a self-contained political unit, with civil affairs generally directed by a governor, assisting officers, and a council of leaders, while the priesthood controls religious and ceremonial matters. In prehistoric times the priests governed all aspects of pueblo life, and even today they select the secular leaders in some of the pueblos. The Pueblos are not organized as a single tribal unit, but they do participate in an All-Pueblo Council, which discusses matters of concern to all of them collectively.

Among the Pueblo Indians, men did the spinning and weaving. This is also the custom in Mexico and Central and South America, even today. Many times, in the author's travels, he has observed the men in the fields of Meso and South America spinning yarn while caring for their flocks.

The prehistoric southwestern culture reached its zenith among the ancient Pueblos. Their descendants can be seen in the villages scattered across New Mexico in an arc, from Zuni, northeast to the Rio Grande Valley as far as Taos.

The Pueblo house is built out of stone and cemented with adobe clay, often several stories high. For defensive purposes, the homes might even be built without doors on the ground level. Sometimes they chose to use ladders leading to the upper level only, which could be pulled up into their dwellings in time of trouble, with the only entry being through the roof.

The author has always been fascinated with the similarity in structure of the Pueblo houses and those found in Old Jerusalem.

Reconstructed ancient Pueblo dwelling, descendants of the Anasazi, from Zuni to Taos, New Mexico.

Casa Rinconada, a great kiva (ceremonial center), Anasazi, A.D. 100 to A.D. 1200, Chaco Canyon, 96 miles north of Gallup, New Mexico.

Chaco Canyon Indians
(96 miles north of Gallup, New Mexico)

Chaco Canyon is found in northwestern New Mexico. If the traveler goes south off New Mexico 17 at Bloomfield, drives 28 miles on New Mexico 44, and follows an unpaved road at Blanco Trading post for 30 miles, he will reach the Chaco Canyon. From the south, turn north on New Mexico 57 from US 66 at Thoreau and proceed 64 miles to the south entrance of the monument. It is wise to check at the Blanco Trading Post or Crownpoint to make sure the unpaved road is passable, if it has been raining. It is worth the trip to see a dozen large pueblos and about 2,000 smaller sites. Travelers may enjoy the experience more if they visit the museum display and dioramas first.

The Anasazi occupied Chaco Canyon from about A.D. 1 to A.D. 1200. Bands of hunters and gatherers roamed the area several thousand years B.C. Farming followed. From this prehistoric people, three groups emerged, and by A.D. 800, one of these groups became the Pueblo civilization—the remains of which we see today.

One of the more notable traits that marked the Pueblo culture was the development of a flat-roofed house of mud, rock, and poles above the ground, in rows and clusters of small rectangular rooms. Each community had one or more small circular semi-subterranean rooms called Kivas used for ceremonial purposes. The great kivas were the center of their religious life—the largest being the Casa Rinconada, which is 64 feet in diameter. Their pottery was a distinctive black on white, and they practiced weaving of cotton textiles.

The largest of these pueblos is the Pueblo Bonito, which is four stories high, with 800 rooms on a floor plan covering three acres. As many as 1,000 people may have inhabited this structure. The logs used for beams still show the effects of the stone axes as they cut into the wood. The sandstone slabs are still in place where women knelt to grind their corn. Some of the plastered walls still bear the fingerprints of the builders. Some of their major building projects include complex irrigation systems and an elaborate network of roads.

They apparently welcomed new people into their community, but the location may have been selected with defense in mind. It was a good place to live. The ponderosa pines that were present in their times have now disappeared, but in their day they enjoyed pine forests on the mesas. There was water at the bottom of the canyon, and crops flourished in the area. But by the 12th century the forests had been destroyed through their use as beams and ceilings in building their homes and for fuel. Without the trees to hold the moisture in the soil, the devastating erosion of the land began and it became useless for farming. So these people abandoned their great buildings, which gradually filled up with dirt and silt.

When a military expedition came upon these mounds in 1849 the city was covered, but indications of a past civilization were there, and artists Richard and Edward Kern drew valuable pictures and maps of the site. The first serious excavation in Chaco Canyon took place between 1896 and 1900. The Navajos came in the 1700s and still occupy much of the surrounding area today.[30]

Pueblo Bonita, 800 rooms, 1,000 inhabitants, Chaco Canyon, 96 miles north of Gallup, New Mexico.

A Chicicahua Appache wickiup, Anadarko, Oklahoma.

An Apache steam bath, Anadarko, Oklahoma.

Apache Indians

Known as fierce warriors and powerful adversaries against their enemies, the Apaches were hardy survivors in a harsh environment. Some historians say the word *Apache* is a Zuni word for "enemy," while others maintain it stems from a Ute or Yavapai word meaning "the people." Many of us remember the early tales of raiding parties and years of bitter fighting with the Apaches against the U.S. Army. In fact, the Army made the name so well known that when many people said "Indian" they meant "Apache."

They are said to be descendants of the Athabaskan bands who came from the north, and were known by the sixteenth century. They capitalized on the use of horses, making it possible in their raids to strike quickly and effectively. They were hunters and not interested in farming—living entirely off the lands containing wild game in the territories of southwest New Mexico, southeastern Arizona, and the northern part of Old Mexico. Simple brush or grass-covered "wickiups" were home to the Apache. These simple huts were built to protect the brave's family from the sun. By throwing a few skins over the framework, they could also protect their family from the rain. The father usually slept out in the open. The Apaches also built their version of a steam bath made of logs and mud. The men would huddle inside this tiny wickiup steam lodge and throw water on the hot stones, heated from the family fire outside.

Geronimo, a Chiricahua Apache warrior, was the last leader of the organized Indian resistance in the United States. His band became one of the most feared in Arizona, raiding back and forth across the U.S. and Mexican border. He was a free spirit who could not endure confinement. In his own words:

We were reckless of our lives, because we felt that every man's hand was against us. If we returned to the reservation we would be put in prison and killed; if we stayed in Mexico they would continue to send soldiers to fight us; so we gave no quarter to anyone and asked no favors.[31]

Once, during a siege led by General Nelson A. Miles, it required five thousand American troops to capture 38 Chiricahua Apaches. Geronimo finally surrendered in August of 1886, spending the rest of his life as a prisoner in Fort Sill, Oklahoma, until his death in 1909. The Apache people wanted only what we prize dearly: freedom.[32]

Cochise was another widely-known Apache leader of the Chiricahua Apaches, living specifically around the Dragoon and Chiricahua mountains of southern Arizona.

The drive that once created the powerful Apache warriors today translates into their being one of the most progressive Indian groups. In barely two generations, and against overwhelming difficulties, they have adjusted to a rather foreign lifestyle and new ways of living. Their ability as stockmen has brought them considerable prosperity. More than 200,000 cattle graze on their reservation. In the month of September, a traveler might be able to witness one of the long Apache cattle drives heading for Whiteriver, McNary and Apache Springs. They also operate a large sawmill at Whiteriver.

Fort Apache Indian Reservation is in the beautiful White Mountains of east-central Arizona, covering over a million-and-a-half acres. It is now being developed as a major recreation area by the White Mountain Apache Tribe. Millions of dollars from tribal funds have gone into the construction of new access roads, 26 mountain lakes and hundreds of campsites. A sports complex near Sunrise Lake will be one of the largest winter resorts in Arizona. This makes the author very proud and pleased when he sees the Indians use their ever-important self-determination to improve their quality of life.

On this reservation are prehistoric ruins that predate the Apache culture. One may ask for directions at Whiteriver, their tribal capital. Hundreds of ruins may be seen, including brush wickiups and quite elaborate cliff dwellings. Very few of the ruins have been excavated, and the visitor, of course, is forbidden to disturb any of them, but is free to pick up arrowheads if they are found on the surface.

The Apache Indians left no markings on stone, but it was said of them that no one fought more bravely than the Apache. Their definition of a reservation was "a large jail where Indians starve and go cold."

Wupatki Ruins
(32 miles north of Flagstaff, Arizona)

Traveling north on U.S. 89, one can find the Wupatki-Sunset Crater entrance, then continue 14 miles eastward to the Visitors' Center.

In A.D. 1065 a great volcano erupted and created what is now known as Sunset Crater (18 miles from the monument headquarters by the Loop Road). The cinders from this explosion spread over 800 square miles. Instead of devastating the land, the lava dust formed a form of mulch which had the ability to conserve moisture, promoting plant growth and enriching the soil. This phenomenon encouraged Indian farmers to move onto the land, and thus came the Anasazi, the Hohokam, the Mogollon and the Patayan, to share the land with the Sinagua who were living there during the eruption. This area became a melting pot for Indian groups—learning and sharing their cultures with each other for over 150 years. They abandoned the land around A.D. 1225.

The name *Wupatki* is a Hopi word meaning "tall house," referring to the multi-story dwelling which was built by the Sinagua Indians (a Pueblo group) during the 12th century. It is four stories high with more than 100 rooms, housing about 200 people. It contained storage bins, metates and manos. The amphitheater, though very likely a dance plaza, resembles in many ways the Kiva of the neighboring Hopis. The ball court found at Wupatki bears a dramatic resemblance to the famous ancient ball courts found in Mexico and South America.

Wukoki Ruins, A.D. 1065-A.D. 1225, 32 miles north of Flagstaff, Arizona.

Lomaki Ruins, A.D. 1065–A.D. 1225, 32 miles north of Flagstaff, Arizona.

Wukoki and Lomaki Ruins
(Near Flagstaff, Arizona

Also part of the Wupatki culture, the Wukoki ruin is a three-story pueblo built out of sandstone during the same period.

The Lomaki ruins, located nearby, are also of this same Wukoki tribe, with a similar dating.

The author was quite impressed with their workmanship. Apparently considerable care was exercised in their construction. Obviously, they were not nomadic wanderers, judging from their sturdy homes.

The Pima and Papago Indian
(Near Phoenix, Arizona)

The Papago and Pima Indians of southern Arizona are believed to be descendants of the Hohokam culture, which reached its peak even earlier than the pueblo-building Anasazi. The *Hohokam*—a Pima word for "those who have vanished"—were famed for their achievements in constructing extensive irrigation systems and canals as far back as A.D. 700.

Some of the most beautiful examples of Indian basketry is made in quantity by the Pima and Papago Indians.

Today, the Pimas live near Phoenix, and the Papagos on a large reservation west of Tucson, Arizona. There is an excellent Indian school and museum in Phoenix. The school, established in 1891, is one of the southwest's oldest and largest Indian boarding schools—accommodating more than a thousand students from the Hopi, Papago, Navajo, Pima, Apache, and Colorado River Reservations.

An ancient Hohokam ruin called Casa Grande is found between Phoenix and Tucson. It contains six prehistoric villages, built around 1350, with thick walls and deep foundations—some having been excavated. When a Spanish padre, Father Kino, found this site in 1694 he named it *Casa Grande,* which is Spanish for "big house." It was abandoned in 1450.

Another prehistoric ruin of the Hohokam-Salado period are found in three sites within easy access to Phoenix and the Pima, Papago reservations.

Navajo National Monument Ruins
(Northeast of Tuba City, Arizona)

These three well-preserved prehistoric dwellings represent the peak of the Anasazi pueblo-dwelling civilization. Known as Betatakin, Keet Seel and Inscription House, they were built in the latter part of the 1200s and abandoned by 1300. They may be reached by traveling 50 miles northeast from Tuba City on U.S. 164 to a paved 9-mile road which branches northward to monument headquarters. If one begins a tour at the museum, it will introduce the visitor to the culture of the Kayenta Anasazi—a branch of the same people who built the dwellings at Mesa Verde and Chaco Canyon.

Keet Seel, built by the Spider Clan, is the largest cliff pueblo in Arizona, containing more than 160 rooms. The traveler can reach this ruin by horseback, traveling 16 miles in all, north from Betatakin, Arizona. The monument superintendent would need to be notified a day before the trip.

Betatakin was built at the opening of a huge cave. One can (with the help of a park ranger) climb down the canyon along a stone stairway and examine the 135 rooms. It is challenging but worth the trip if the traveler is in good health.

Inscription house (30 miles from monument headquarters), built by the Snake Clan, is definitely for those who enjoy hiking, and can be reached in a five-mile round trip. Be sure to ask the ranger for directions and register upon leaving and returning.

Aztec Ruins, circa A.D. 1124, Aztec, Cortez, Colorado (Four Corners area).

Aztec Ruins National Monument
(North of Aztec, New Mexico)

The San Juan River and its tributaries drain the region known as the Four Corners country—the area surrounding the point where New Mexico, Colorado, Utah and Arizona meet in a common boundary at right angles. Aztec lies between two major Anasazi areas—Mesa Verde and Chaco Canyon. Located on the Animas River, it is twenty miles below the Colorado state line.

Covering 27 acres, this enormous ruin (built 800 years ago) was once a prehistoric town built like an apartment surrounding a plaza. It is obvious that they were an industrious and cooperative people. Without a great degree of organization and leadership, these complex buildings would have been impossible. The 500 rooms rise to two and three stories in some parts. There are a number of sacred kivas within the building and a larger ceremonial kiva central to a number of small rooms. The Great Kiva has been restored for visitors to see. They were very religious, with almost every thought and act in their daily lives influenced by the supernatural powers which they believed ruled their universe.

This area was occupied first by the Chaco-like people, who abandoned the city around A.D. 1124, and at another period by the Mesa Verde group. The second occupation by the Mesa Verde group was more ambitious, setting local cobblestones in adobe mortar to build their homes. They lived there for only 25 or 30 years and then abandoned the area for unknown reasons. It now contains six major archaeological complexes and at least seven smaller unexcavated mounds.

Lost City, Nevada
(Moapa Valley, Nevada)

The Lost City, or the Pueblo Grande de Nevada, is located on the muddy River banks in Moapa Valley, near what is now called the Valley of Fire in Nevada. A museum located at

Overton, sixty miles northeast of Las Vegas, provides a history of the people who once inhabited this valley. A reconstruction of original pueblo dwellings, as well as displays of the pottery, basketweaving, farming methods and warfare, are on display. Petroglyphs are featured, accompanied by possible interpretations. The glyphs on one of the stones greatly resemble one of the lost ancient forms of writing, known as *ogam*.

The Lost City people buried their dead under the floors of their homes, along with their possessions. Farming seemed to be their chief occupation, and they used the process of irrigation to produce their beans, squash, cotton, and corn. It is believed that drought, famine and disease may have driven them northward.

The height of this civilization was believed to be about A.D. 800, with the Pueblos leaving in a hurry around A.D. 1000. Later the Paiutes replaced them as hunters and gatherers. Then early pioneer farmers replaced the Paiutes, and their descendants still live there today.

Petroglyphs, Lost City, Pueblo Grande de Nevada, A.D. 800–A.D. 1000. Moapa Valley, Nevada (east of Las Vegas).

Petroglyphs, Lost City, Pueblo Grande de Nevada, A.D. 800–A.D. 1000. Moapa Valley, Nevada (east of Las Vegas).

Reconstruction, original Pueblo dwelling, Lost City, Nevada.

CALIFORNIA AREA

Yuma, Chumash, Shasta and Pomo Indians

Indian civilizations in prehistoric times were more dense in California than in many other parts of America north of Mexico. Some scholars believe that 150,000 people were living in the area now called California when the Spanish arrived, and may have numbered as high as 300,000 at the zenith of their civilization. But the population diminshed, partially, through conflict and disease brought by the white settlers.

The acorn was the staff of life, and fish, with various nuts, berries and fruit, made their survival quite easy.

A tribe called the Chumash lived on islands in and around Santa Barbara. The Shasta tribe lived north near the Oregon line. The Salinans lived south of Monterey.

The lower Colorado River was the home of the Yumas, the only farmers in the California area. The Pomo, who lived north of San Francisco, were specialists in basketweaving—some even made with feathers and beads.

California State Indian Museum

(Sutter's Fort, Sacramento, California)

The visitor can find this facility on 2701 L Street, on the grounds of Sutter's Fort in Sacramento, California. This museum is completely devoted to the life of California Indians, present and past, and includes many archaeological displays. A special feature is at Hospital Rock in Sequoia, where a prehistoric village site is seen, along with rock art.

Clear Lake State Park

Traveling from Lakeport on California 29, driving south on local Kelseyville, northeast four miles on Soda Bay Road, the visitor can reach the park entrance.

Here the prehistoric Indians lived much the same as the Pomo Indians who once had a settlement by this lake. Archaeologists have found a sweathouse, which was apparently very important to ancient Indian life—an earth-covered structure, smaller than their dwellings. The men came to a sweathouse in ancient times, much as men today go to clubs. They were used for fellowship and conversation rather than for reasons of health.

A ceremonial house was also found at Clear Lake—built much like the sweathouse but much larger. It was here that the people gathered for dances and religious ceremonies. California Indians never developed a religious priesthood. They did, however, have medicine men and two major cults called Kuksu and Toloache. Although California Indians spoke many different languages, their ceremonial rituals were similar.

Randall Museum
(San Francisco, California)

Located at 199 Museum Way, The Josephine D. Randall Junior Museum is designed primarily as a teaching aid for school children. One display features prehistoric artifacts found in a Costanoan shell mound, demonstrating the techniques used in excavation. The museum has reconstructed the myths, stories and pattern of social order from the accounts left by early Spanish missionaries. The museum had, with the cooperation of the San Francisco State College Department of Anthropology, offered young people the opportunity of digging in an archaeological site, finding artifacts and recording the information.

Museum of Natural History
(Los Angeles, California)

Located in Exposition Park, at 900 West Exposition Boulevard, the visitor will find exhibits dating back to the earliest known datings. There are dioramas demonstrating how the Indians made their baskets, blankets, stone tools and pottery. A Chumash village on the coast is also reproduced, with models illustrating other aspects of prehistoric life in California. This museum has even included displays from the Hohokam and Anasazi cultures in the southwest.

San Diego Museum of Man
(Balboa Park, San Diego, California)

This museum possesses rich resources of southern California and Southwestern material, and the exhibits change frequently. Two cultures are featured—San Diequito and Diegueno. *San Diequito* refers to a very early culture, and *Diegueno* is a later group extending into historic times. The Diegueno Indians have lived in the San Diego area for the last thousand years. They introduced the art of pottery making, and also practice cremation of their dead. The museum also includes an extensive collection of bows and arrows, with examples from North, Central and South America.

There are many other fine museums in California. The author has only mentioned a few, as it was impossible for him to visit all of them in his research—the main thesis being that a great many Indians lived in North America in prehistoric times, with California being one of the most heavily populated areas.

PLATEAU AREA

Nez Perce, Yakima, Walla Walla and Palouse Indians

Westward from the Shoshoni mountain and ranging over much of Idaho and the eastern sections of Washington and Oregon, lived a group of neighboring tribes, speaking varying dialects of a related language known as Shahaptian. These tribes included the Nez Perce (pronounced *nez purs*), meaning, "pierced nose" (although very few Indians ever followed this practice). It was a name given to the group in 1805 by a Frenchman who gave them this name after seeing some of the tribe members wearing shells in their noses as a form of decoration.

The Nez Perce resisted the efforts of the government to place them on reservations. Chief Joseph tried to lead a band of their group into Canada, but finally surrendered at the U.S.-Canadian border.

When the Indians were struggling to keep their lands, some of the chiefs quickly recognized the military strength of the white men. One of the more remarkable Indian leaders was Chief Joseph, the last great leader of the Nez Perce. He struggled valiantly to remain at peace with the whites, but was, in the end, forced to become the military leader for the Nez Perce, in their last effort to retain their traditional way of life.

Chief Joseph was born in the Wallowa Valley of Oregon in 1840, the son of a local leader and chief. In his youth he attended a missionary school near his home—his father being extremely interested in the teachings of Christianity. In fact, the name *Joseph* was given him by one of the missionaries, the name meaning "Thunder Over the Land."

When Joseph succeeded his father as leader of his band he knew the military power of the whites was so great that they would never be able to achieve a final victory over them should they go to war. When his beloved Wallowa Valley was confiscated, Joseph began moving his band of 350 warriors, women and children northward. In an effort to retain their independence and traditional life-style, they fought eleven battles against a total of two thousand white troops armed with artillery and the best rifles. The Indian warriors finally surrendered and the entire band was placed in Fort Leavenworth, Kansas. Later they were moved to the Indian territory of Oklahoma. After many long years, the remnants of the band were finally allowed to return to their beloved Northwest. It was here that Chief Joseph lived until his death in 1904. He spent the last years of his life encouraging his people to adjust to the white man's way of life.[33] These people became friendly to the white man and have a reputation for seeking the white man's knowledge—even sending some of their young men to their schools.

The Yakima, Walla Walla, and Palouse tribes were also from this general area of the Northwest.

NORTH PACIFIC COAST AREA

Nootka Indians

On March 28, 1778, John Ledyard (part of Captain Cook's Pacific expedition) became one of the first white men to land on the Northwest Coast. Because he was especially interested in Indians, having once lived for some time among the Iroquois in the Northeast, he was fascinated with the Nootka village which he found after having sailed halfway around the world from New England. Quoting from his journal (with the spelling intact), he wrote:

It was a matter of doubt with many of us whether we should find any inhabitants here, but we had scarcely entered the inlet before we saw that hardy, that intriped, that glorious creature man approaching us from the shore...In the evening we were visited by several canoes full of natives ...The country around this sound is generally high and mountainous...intirely covered with woods...We saw no plantations or any appearance that exhibited any knowledge of the cultivation of the earth, all seemed to remain in a state of nature...We purchased while here about 1500 beaver, besides other skins, but took none but the best ...Neither did we purchas a quarter part of the beaver and other furr skins we might have done...

Ledyard described the canoes as he continued:

They are about 20 feet in length, contracted at each end, and about three feet broad in the middle...made from large...trees.... I had no sooner beheld these Americans than I set them down for the same kind of people that inhabited the opposide side of the continent.[34]

No people in America had the variety of food as did the Indians of the Pacific coast from northern California to southern Alaska. They enjoyed shellfish, salmon, halibut, cod, herring, and candle-fish. Great quantities of sea mammals were available to them as well as the land animals and birds. Some consider the Northwest Coast Indians even wealthy by prehistoric standards.

The Northwest Coast people were marvelous on several counts. They produced a genuinely high culture which ranked with the Pueblos of the Southwest. They were a motivated people who placed a high value on acquisition of private property. They were a seagoing people, specializing in the fishing of salmon, cod and halibut—securing enough through spring and summer to feed them through the winter months. The Nootka tribe was particularly known for their long boats used for harpooning whales.

Extended families lived together in plank houses—the posts and door poles being carved and painted with their family crest. This custom eventually developed into the now-famous monuments known as totem poles, with new crests added as the families increased. We also know that some slavery was practiced and some secret societies existed. It was, however, the fur trade which became the bridge between their isolated prehistoric society and civilization as we know it today.

GREAT BASIN AREA

Ute and Paiute Indians

The Utes and Paiutes wandered up and down Utah and eastward into the Colorado Rockies. The Utes called themselves *Nuntz,* meaning "the people." The name Paiute means "the true Utes," or "the Utes that live by the water." The name for the state of Utah comes from the Ute Indians. They were basically a food-gathering, hunting people that divided into small bands and gradually accepted the agricultural life rather than the nomadic existence.

The Utes are now divided into the Southern Ute in southwestern Colorado and the Northern Ute in Duchesne, near Vernal, Utah. Linguistically, the Ute and the Paiute belong to the Shoshoean branch of the Uto-Aztecan stock.

The houses of the early people were cone-shaped and built of brush, reeds and grasses. They also live in tents made of animal skins. Because they disliked farming they lived off seeds and roots, along with fishing and hunting.

The Ute medicine man used yarrow, a flowering sprig, for a salve to heal cuts and bruises. Modern herbologists are beginning to study old Indian remedies and are developing a growing respect for this art, in that herbs and roots were actually mankinds's first medicine.

The modern Ute is an isolationist by nature and would prefer to be left alone. In 1950, the Confederated Ute tribes won a $31,000,000 judgment from the United States, and since then have discovered oil and gas on their lands—enriching the Ute tribal treasuries considerably. Modern homes have been built, health and sanitation standards have improved; new roads are being constructed, and many educational scholarships are being made avalable to young members of the tribe.

Many observers sense a strong revival of interest in Ute culture and ancient customs. The two traditions still adhered to by the progressive Utes are the Bear Dance (welcome to spring), and the Sun Dance (a religious ritual).

There seems to be an attitude of self-determination among the Ute people, with evidence of improved leadership. The Ute Indian people now enjoy the highest standard of living they have ever known in modern times. Along with this progress, it is the author's hope that none of their arts, crafts, kindly traditions, customs and oral traditions will be lost, but proudly continued from one generation to another.

Ute Museum
(Montrose, Colorado)

From Montrose, drive four miles south on U.S. 550. This museum, on the banks of the Uncompahgre River, is situated on a 400-acre farm once owned by Ute Chief Ouray and his wife Chipeta. The museum now rests on six acres of the land—one of the few museums devoted to a single Indian tribe. The bulk of the artifacts were donated by pioneer photographer Tom McKee, and since that time has been enlarged through gifts from the Daughters of the American Revolution.

The Utes once occupied half of what is now known as Colorado, plus two-thirds of Utah and parts of northern New Mexico. Their language was similar to that of the Comanche, Shoshone, and Hopi Indians. The Utes were basically a peaceful tribe, given to hunting and gathering wild foods and dwelling in teepees. Gradually the white man encroached upon their lands until finally the Utes were relegated to a reservation on the western third of Colorado.

Later, with the discovery of gold and silver, the Utes gave up more land for money and gold.

The Paiute (pronounced *pie-yoot*) tribe has two groups—the Northern Paiute and the Southern Paiute—living on reservations throughout Arizona, California, Nevada, Oregon and Utah.

The Northern Paiute once lived near Owens Lake in California, over Nevada and south of the Columbian River in Oregon. The southern Paiute covered the area from the Mohave Desert of California to the Colorado River in Arizona and Northward to central Utah. They were great hunters, choosing to follow the lakes and marshes, also collecting berries, nuts and seeds. They, too, lived in cone-shaped houses of brush, and they more or less worshiped the various powers of nature.

During the 1800s, the Northern Paiute resisted the encroachment of white settlers in the area and won an important victory at Pyramid Lake, Nevada, in 1860. The Southern Paiute, however, have been relatively peaceful, although they were occasionally raided by the Navajo and Ute Indians. It was during the 1860s and 70s that the U.S. government finally established reservations for both groups of Paiute.

North American Indian Mounds

The Indians of ancient America built three types of mounds: (1) temple mounds, built approximately 1,000 years ago, and used for religious purposes: (2) burial mounds, and (3) refuse mounds, where the Indians buried their garbage and refuse.

The temple mounds were built much like those erected in Mexico and Central America: a building constructed on an elevated earthern platform where religious ceremonies and rituals took place. These platform mounds were built as foundations for their temples and other public buildings, and constructed in stages over a period of several generations. Each time a building was replaced, a new layer of earth was added to the mound in basketloads. Some mounds contained thousands of cubic feet of earth.

The first modern recorded histroy on the subject of ancient North American mounds appeared in the writings of the DeSoto expedition, which explored Florida in 1539. The Spanish observed that the mounds had been there for some time—though later, Benjamin Franklin and Noah Webster falsely blamed DeSoto for the building of the mounds.

As the colonial explorers traveled westward and began felling trees and tilling the earth, they discovered numerous mounds and earthworks. Then, at last, when inventory was finally taken among the explorers and historians, it was discovered that there were ancient mounds and earthworks from the Rocky Mountains to the Atlantic Ocean, covering the entire eastern portion of the United States. Some archaeologists estimate that there are some 10,000 mounds in the state of Ohio alone.

The author wishes to end this section with photographs of a beautiful collection of scaled models of early Indian dwellings,[35] and trusts the reader may have become a bit more enlightened regarding prehistoric civilizations in North America. Brief directions also have been included with many of the sites, in the event that some might wish to visit these very accessible areas and learn about them in greater detail.

Again, volumes have and will continue to be written about these fascinating ancient Americans. It is the author's intent, in this chapter, to provide only a brief overview of some of the major prehistoric areas in North America.

Scaled Replicas of Early Indian Dwellings
(Courtesy Robert J. Beckstein, Tacoma, Washington.)

Apache wickiup.

Mud-covered wickiup.

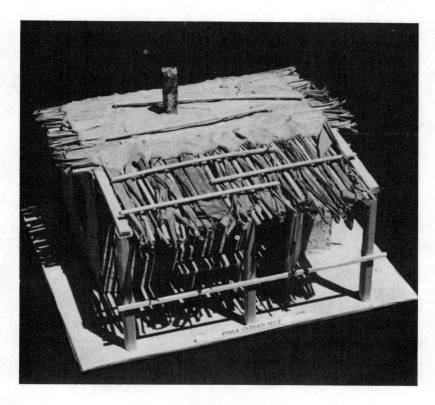

Pima Indian hut.

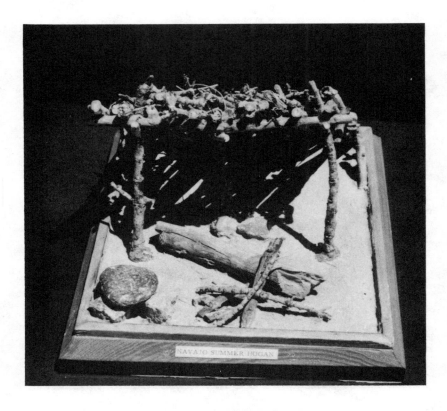

Navajo summer hogan.

Sioux wigwam.

Navajo six-sided hogan.

Hopi pueblo apartment.

Part
Two

2

The Origins of the American Indian

For centuries, the subject of Indian origins has been a source of fascination to scholars and researchers who are still seeking answers to questions regarding the mystery of varying cultures found in ancient America.

The author can remember, as a small child in school, how the teacher displayed a map of the world, pointing out the interesting configurations of the major continents. It was elementary and obvious, she suggested, to observe how the east coast of South America could slide snugly into the west coast of Africa. That teacher and her students were neither the first nor the last to be intrigued by the idea that the continental shelves seemed to fit together like a simple jigsaw puzzle. Soon after the contour of the American continent made its way onto sixteenth century maps, the curiosity of geographers and adventurers was aroused by the apparent relationship of the opposite coasts of the Atlantic ocean. Even Benjamin Franklin and other serious philosophers and scientists occasionally pondered the possibility of the continents being one land mass at some point in history. This idea became known as the theory of Continental Drift.

Ten years after an elementary teacher had stirred his imagination, the notion of drifting continents again was impressed upon the author's mind by a geography professor in college, who presented this theory as a fairy tale. As a matter of fact, until the scientific revolution (which began in this century) placed the concept within the realm of possibility, scientists considered a mobility of land masses not only impossible, but ridiculous.

The first trace of credibility emerged from the work of Alfred Wegener, a German meteorologist who, at the beginning of the twentieth century, demonstrated the similarities of fossils and rocks on the opposite sides of the Atlantic. Believing the earth to have been joined at one time, he named his theoretical land mass *Pangaea,* meaning "all lands," and the huge sea which washed its shores, *Panthalassa,* meaning "all seas." He compared the two continents to pieces of torn newspaper on which, when refit, the lines of print run smoothly across. His metaphor and painstaking research were ignored or ridiculed for a quarter of a century. Later, impressive collections of fossilized bones, plant remains, and skeletal imprints from widely distributed areas finally convinced many scientists that the continents must have been joined sometime in the remote past. However, sufficient evidence to persuade the doubters in the scientific community did not accumulate until 1965.[1]

Now, as research has progressed and the theory of plate tectonics has developed (the offspring of the Continental Drift theory), the idea of the great original land mass separating into two enormous continents is being considered more seriously.

The Bible teaches in the beginning all the water was in one place. It therefore follows that all the land was in one place (see Genesis 1:9).

According to the Bible, the creation of this earth was divided into periods of time. During one of these eras God said *"Let the waters under the heaven be gathered together unto one place and let the dry land appear: and it was so"* (see Genesis 1:9). Evidently, from the beginning when Adam and Eve were placed in the Garden of Eden, the water was in one place on the earth and the land was in another.

The scriptures give no further indication of a change in the land structure until an obscure phrase in the Bible mentioned a man named Peleg, saying *in his days the earth was divided.* (see Chronicles 1:19, Genesis 10:25).

Some skeptics say this passage indicates a political, nation-by-nation division of the earth, rather than a geological occurrence. Today, however, respected theologians believe this verse refers to the actual physical creation of the Atlantic Ocean.

To substantiate Genesis 10:25, which documents the earth as being divided in the days of Peleg, Dr. Immanuel Velikovsky explains:

> The theory of drifting continents, debated since the 1920's has its starting point in the similarity of the shape of the coastlines of Brazil and Africa. This similarity (or better, complementation), plus some early fauna and floral affinities suggested to Professor Wegener. . .that in the early geological age these two continents, South American and Africa, were one land mass. But since animal and vegetable affinities could also be found in other parts of the world, Wegener conjectured that all continents and islands were once a single land mass that in various epochs divided and drifted apart. Those who do not subscribe to the theory of Continental Drift continue to explain the affinity of plants and animals by theories of "land bridges" or former land connections between continents and also between continents and islands.[2]

With regard, then, to the theory of Continental Drift, or the division of the earth, the technology of science is beginning to correlate with the Biblical record, as is often the case. However, a great deal of disagreement still exists as to how and when the division of the single continent took place. Two major possibilities, among others, are (1) that the continents, over thousands of years, gradually drifted apart, or (2) that some cataclysmic or celestial power caused a sudden division during the lifetime of one man.

Some scientists believe the separation of the continents took place progressively, over a period of approximately two hundred million years, and further suggest that today's ocean floor is still spreading, moving North American one inch farther from Europe every year. They project that in fifty million years the land around the Mediterranean Sea will have closed in from all sides to form a large lake; that Africa will have begun to break apart, and part of California will detach from the mainland.[3]

If one takes the scriptures literally, the physical division of the earth took place during the lifetime of Peleg, a descendant of Noah.

How long after the flood did the division take place? In Genesis, the generations of men after Noah are listed and the ancestry of Peleg given:

> These are the generations of Shem: Shem was an hundred years old, and begat Arphaxad two years after the flood: And Shem lived after he begat Arphaxad five hundred years, and begat sons and daughters. And Arphaxad...begat Salah:...and Salah lived thirty years, and begat Eber...and Peleg...begat Reu: And Peleg lived after he begat Reu two hundred and nine years, and begat sons and daughters. (see Genesis 11:10-19).

The chronology of the Bible suggests the earth was divided quickly and dramatically during the lifetime of Peleg; a time that can be approximated at 2300 B.C. Although this places the division of the earth as occurring nearly 4300 years ago, such dating is definitely at odds with science. Their theory of a gradual division is in direct conflict with the Biblical account, which suggests an unexplained force or power accelerated the earth's division in a much shorter time period as that allowed by science for Continental Drift. A supernatural or cataclysmic occurrence could explain this division as described in the scriptures.

Since the scriptures indicate the division took place in the days of Peleg, from the evidence in Genesis this action occurred between 101 and 340 years after the Flood. Therefore, after the Flood, the earth remained a single land mass for a minimum of 101 years and a maximum of 340 years. Consequently, after the Flood, while the earth was still one continent, would it not be possible for the animals and some of Noah's descendants to wander to the portion of the continent now known as the New World? In other words, if we follow this line of thinking, the Indians may not have been the first group (after the Flood) to be on the land we now call America.

This unresolved problem of chrononlogy creates additional questions regarding the peopling of the New World. For example, anyone traveling in the Mississippi or Ohio Valleys today would see how scientific excavations have unearthed skeletal remains, pottery, and other remnants of human existence, along with a scientific explanation of the original people of the American continent. A visitor is told that certain "Indiana" or ancestors of the Indian came over the Bering Strait about 8000 B.C., and became the first inhabitants. They would also speculate concerning other aspects of their origins and culture.

Migrations

Scholars theorize those coming across the Bering Strait might have traveled both eastward through the United States, and southward through Mexico, Central and South America. With this thought in mind, the author has, for the past 30 years, traveled many thousands of miles throughout the United States, Mexico, Central and South America, cataloging research and photographs which might determine migratory links and patterns of the Indians of the Americas. Did they come from the Bering Strait only, or did they come from the south, landing on the east or west coast; or, might any combination of all these possibilities be true? The study becomes so complicated that, at best, our efforts can be only fragmentary.

Origins

The following information has been gleaned from many years of research and field experience on this subject:

Northwestern University archaeologists believe the Indians who lived in the central Mississippi River Valley in 6500 B.C. were not primitive savages. These aborigines left evidences of a rather sophisticated people who utilized their environment well and developed an effective strategy for survival. (See Beth S. King, *New York Times*, June 16, 1975.)

Some walls of a ruin known as Mystery Hill, in New Hampshire, have been dated at 2000 B.C. After extensive investigation, comparing this Pre-Columbian civilization with similar Old World examples, researchers still puzzle over these ancient Americans who understood such advanced techniques in stonework.[4]

Racial Mixtures

Pedro de Cieza de Leon, a Spanish soldier-writer and recognized chronicler of pre-Columbian history, wrote of the Colla Indians and how they told him of a pre-Inca race of bearded white men living near Lake Titicaca until they were exterminated.[5]

Indeed, white people have been mentioned also in the writings of the great Mexican chroniclers, Fray Bernardino de Sahagun and Juan de Torquemada. Sahagun wrote of the ancient Totonoes in Mexico:

All the men and women are white, with good, well dis-
posed faces, with good features; their language was very
different than others, although some spoke Otomi, some
Nahuatl, and there are others that understand the Huaxteca
tongue. And they are curious and skilled in song; they
dance gracefully with beautiful movements.[6]

Sahagun continues as he describes the Huaxteca group:

This name comes from Pantla or Panotla
[Panuco],...for Pantla is also the name of the place where
they dwell. Pantla...means "where the water is crossed,"
for this is on the sea coast.

Hence it is given the name, "where the water is crossed:
they say those who arrived,...who settled here in the land
called Mexico...came in boats; they crossed over the sea.[7]

Sahagun then mentions the Mexica group:

In the distant past,...the ones who came
[first],...those who came to rule in this land,...came over
the water in boats; [they came] in many divisions. And
they drew along the coast, the coast to the north. And where
they came to beach their boats is named...Pantla.[8]

Juan de Torquemada wrote of a people who came to Tula,
Mexico, whose leader was white: "It is well known that he was
of a very good disposition, white, blond, bearded and with good
features."[9]

He continued:

There came from toward the North certain nations of
peoples, who disembarked by Panuco [Tampico, Mexico].
These people were of good carriage, well dressed in long
robes like the Turks, or in black linen like the cassocks
of the clergy, open in front, without capes, low-cut at the
neck, and with short, wide sleeves which did not reach
below the elbow.[10]

Essentially, these writings told of a caucasian people
who migrated to ancient America by sea.

In the Maya context, Fray Diego de Landa (1524-1597), one of the early Spanish padres, recorded a Yucatan tradition concerning their forefathers which links them to the Middle East:

> Some of the old people of Yucatan say that they have
> heard from their ancestors that this land was occupied by
> a race of people, who came from the East and whom God
> had delivered by opening twelve paths through the sea.

If this were true, it necessarily follows that all the inhabitants of the Indies are descendants of the Jews.[11]

The Cakchiquel Maya tribe, neighbors to the Quiche, had once belonged to the same Indian group. They also had common oral traditions which had been preserved for generations. Several members of the Xahil family recorded them near the end of the sixteenth century. The narrative of their first forebearers was in harmony with the Quiche record:

> I shall write the stories of our first fathers and
> grandfathers, one of whom was called *Gagavitz,* the other
> *Zactecauh:* the stories that they told to us; that from the
> other side of the sea we come to the place called Tulan,
> where we were begotten and given birth by our mothers
> and our fathers...[12]

An ancient American Indian prince named Fernando de Alva Ixtililxochitl (eesht-*leel*-sho-*sheetl*) wrote a very valuable history of his people and their traditions, in his native tongue. When the Spanish Padres arrived in the New World, the prince's writings were translated into a modern tongue, and thus became a priceless record for us to study. He wrote of three groups of people who inhabited this land, the first nation being the *Chichimecs:*

> It is the common and general opinion of the natives of
> this Chichimec land, which is now called New Spain,
> besides that it appears in their historical picture writings,
> that their forefathers came from Western lands.[13]

He described the second group:

And the Toltecs...came to these parts, having first passed over great lands and seas, living in caves and passing through great hardships, until getting to this land.[14]

Of the third nation he wrote:

Those who possessed the New World in this third age were the Olmecs and Zicalancas, and according to what is found in their histories, *they came in ships or barges from the East to the land of Potonchan (Tobasco)* from which they began to settle.[15]

This royal prince Ixtililxochitl of Texcoco made a noteworthy correlation with the scriptural account of the dispersion of peoples after the Tower of Babel (see Genesis 11:1-9):

The men made a very high and strong Zacualli, which means very high tower, to protect themselves in it when the second world would be destroyed. At the best time their languages were confounded, and not understanding one another, they went away to different parts of the world.[16]

When Hernando Cortez conquered Mexico, their great native Aztec leader, Montezuma, surprised the Spanish explorer with the following response:

For a long time we have known from the writings of our ancestors that neither I, nor any of those who dwell in this land, are natives of it, but foreigners who came from very different parts; and likewise we know that a chieftain, of whom they were all vassals, brought our people to this region. And he returned to his native land and after many years came again, by which time all those who had remained were married to native women and had built villages and raised children. And when he wished to lead them away again they would not go nor even admit him as their chief; and so he departed. And we have always held that those who descended from him would come and

conquer this land and take us as their vassals. So because
of the place from which you claim to have come, namely,
from where the sun rises, and the things you tell us of the
great lord or king who sent you here, we believe and are
certain that he is our natural lord, especially as you say
that he has known of us for some time. So be assured that
we shall obey you and hold you as our lord in place of
that great sovereign of whom you speak; and in this there
shall be no offense or betrayal whatsoever. And in all the
land that lies in my domain, you may command as you
will, for you shall be obeyed; and all that we own is for
you to dispose of as you choose.[17]

Montezuma later told some of his leaders:

I also believe that your own ancestors must have handed
down to you the record that we are not natives of this land
but come to it from another very distant country, led by
the lord. . .and you well know that we have always expected
this lord, and now, from what the Captain has told us. . .and
because of the region from which he says he came, I hold
it for certain and you should do the same, that this King
(of Spain) is the lord we expected.[18]

Cortez records the following in his writings:

Montezuma replied that. . .they were not natives of the
land but had come to it a long time since and. . .were well pre-
ared to believe that they erred somewhat from the true faith
during the long time since they had left their native land.[19]

R.A. Jairazbhoy also wrote of Asians coming to pre-
Columbian America:

As many as 41 particular instances of Japanese junks
drifting onto the American coast were recorded in less than
a century following 1782. Only twelve among these were
deserted. The survivors, all men, settled for the most part
in the region where they had been washed ashore.[20]

Jairazbhoy's basic conclusion was almost every major development in any area of the world had its roots elsewhere, as was the case in India and Japan. However, the people who settled in the New World appear to have been welcomed, possibly because of their new ideas.[21]

Modern studies reveal evidence of Oriental blood, but that alone did not make them what they were. The magnificent carvings found in wood, stone, and pottery throughout Mexico, Central and South America are reminiscent in styles to those of Egypt, Greece, Assyria, Japan and China. Indeed, we may say that the ancient Americans, in many instances, were a cosmopolitan race.

An observing, scientific mind might analyze the problem and ask pertinent questions, as did writer M.C. Lorang:

It would have been a joy to tell from whence the peoples of Mayan America came. We can be certain some came from Asia, but from where did the Olmecs come? And where did they go? Why are sculptures from thirteeth-century Cambodia similar to Vera Cruz Olmec heads, older than 600 B.C.? Why do carved stones from Tiquisate, Guatemala, have a laughing and a sad side, reminiscent of Greek stage decorations? Why do statuettes from fifth-century Oaxaca resemble Shakespearean jesters? Why do figurines from the Gulf coast make one think of effervescent movie actors? Is Dr. Sidney Edelstein right in thinking the similarity of dyes used in Mexico and Israel (I might add Pliny's Rome) has a bearing on Mayan migration? If so, which way did the migration go, from Israel to Rome to Middle America or vice versa?[22]

Sir Grafton Elliot Smith, a chief spokesman and anatomist wrote of studies which seemed to trace all civilization back to Egypt:

...whence it was carried...all over the world by sun-worshipping, gold-seeking Egyptians...spreading out from

Egypt, [they] first came to Mesopotamia, where they built or taught the natives to build ziggurats in imitation of their own pyramids. Later they repeated the performance in Cambodia and finally in Central America.[23]

In South America stories persist concerning their origins, which link them not only with the Old World, but particularly to the Middle East, with oral traditions and stories very similar to the great flood described in the Old Testament. Father Jose de Acorta, a Spanish padre of the Colonial era, recorded the following traditions, which parallel histories in both the Old and the New Worlds:

It is no matter of any great importance to know what the Indians themselves report of their beginning, being more like unto dreams than to true histories. They make great mention of a deluge which happened in their country. . . The Indians say that all men were drowned in this deluge, and they report that out of the great Lake Titicaca came one Viracocha, who stayed in Tiahuanaco, where at this day there is [sic] to be seen the ruins of ancient and very strange buildings, and from thence came to Cuzco, and so began mankind to multiply. They show in the same lake a small island, where they feign that the sun hid himself and so was preserved; and for this reason they make great sacrifices unto him in that place, both of sheep [i.e., llamas] and men.

Others report that six, or I know not what number of men, came out of a certain cave by a window, by whom men first began to multiply; and for this reason they call them Paccari-tambo. And therefore they are of opinion that the Tambos are the most ancient race of men. They say also that Manco Capac, whom they acknowledge for the founder and chief of their Incas, was issued of that race and that from him sprang two families or lineages, the one of Hanan Cuzco and the other of Urin Cuzco. They say, moreover that when the King Incas attempted war and conquered sundry provinces they gave a colour and made a pretext of their enterprise, saying that all the world ought to acknowledge them for that all the world was renewed by their race and country; and also the true religion had been revealed to them from heaven.[24]

The Aztecs taught that their ancestral father and mother, with their fifteen children, came to this land by way of a boat.[25]

Andres de Tapia said that Montezuma told Cortez how the people known as Indians had come from ships. This general tradition among Montezuma's people indicates that the early arrivals were white men with a civilization of Mediterranean origin and with traditions we of today could scarcely fail to assign to Phoenicians, Egyptians and Greeks. There seem to be traces of all these influences in some of the pre-Columbian civilizations.[26]

For years the Aztecs had "been wandering from place to place, seeking a promised land which their diety had offered them."[27]

Other enduring traditions that indicate a Hebrew origin of some of the ancestors of the American Indian are as follows:

In his history of the Indian of the Mississippi, Du Pratz says that an old Indian chief who kept the temple told him that his race came from the south and west—indicating Mexico and the southern region—and that they were driven into this land, and at that time white people filled . . . the entire land with cities and villages. When pressed for an answer from where his people originally came, he said that they did not know, but that their most ancient speech—presumably, says the author, their most ancient legend—says their fathers came from where the sun rises; that they were a long time on their journey and were on the point of perishing in their journey. The Indian further claimed that they reached this land without any effort on their part, implying that some power other than their own brought them

here. He said that their God was most great and powerful; that
he created everything we can see and everything we can't see.
In other words, their God created the heavens and the earth and
all things that are in them.[28]

Although the basic meaning of the Hopi creation myth and
the symbol which expresses it is subjective, we cannot ignore
the literal interpretation—that the Hopis came to America from
across the sea, crossing on boats or rafts from one
"steppingstone," or island, to the next. A similar interpretation
can be made of the myth of the ancient Quiche Maya, which
tells how the waters parted and the tribes crossed on
steppingstones placed in a row over the sand ("stones in a row,
sand under the sea.")[29]

We cannot ignore the oral legends and traditions of these
ancient Americans. Handed down from one generation to
another through tribal story-tellers, they were the means of
preserving priceless genealogies and traditions. Even though
some of the stories may have deteriorated over the centuries
through the telling, they still provide fascinating bits of
information which link them with Christianity and the Old
World, and might even help us find some of the lost pieces to
their cultural puzzle.

Author Lewis Spence quotes a Dr. Starr, who recounts the
surprisingly "Christian" religious traditions of the Cherokees:

They stated that from time immemorial the tribes had
been divided in sentiment; that while the greater part had
been idolatrous—worshipping the sun, moon, stars and
other objects—a small portion denied that system and taught
that there were three beings above who created all things
and will judge all men; that they fixed the time and manner
of death. . . .They sit on three white seats and are the only
objects to which worship and prayers should be directed.
The angels are their messengers and come to earth to attend
to the affairs of men.

They claim that Yehowa was the name of the great king. He was a man, yet a spirit; a great and glorious being. His name was never to be mentioned in common talk. This great king commanded them to rest every seventh day. They were told not to work on this day and that they should devote it to talking about God.

Yehowa created the world in seven days at Nu-ta-te-qua, the first new moon of the Autumn, with the fruits all ripe. God made the first man of red clay and he was an Indian, and made woman of one of his ribs. All people were Indians or red people before the flood. They had teachers and prophets who taught the people to obey God and their parents. They warned the people of the approaching flood, but said that the world would be destroyed by water only once, and that later it would be destroyed by fire, when God would send a shower of pitch and then a shower of fire which would burn up everything. They also taught that after death the good and bad would be separated; the good would take a path that would lead to happiness, where it would always be light; but evil led to a deep chasm.[30]

In his valuable publication, *The History of the American Indians,* James Adair wrote, "The Navajos believe that all Indians and white people lived together at one time, all speaking the same tongue."[31]

Hubert Howe Bancroft wrote of the Algonquins who claim they are of foreign origin and came here by sea, "Anciently they celebrated with an annual thank offering, in remembrance of their ancestors' happy arrival in America."[32]

Sigvald Linne, a respected scholar and researcher, has offered the following opinion regarding ancient Old World connections in early America and also Polynesia:

Archaeologists and ethnologists in America have been seized by the general tendency to eliminate all distances.

Detailed studies are continued with increasing intensity and with more efficient methods, but at the same time remote associations are made, so daring that they would have been considered as jokes a score or so years ago. It is considered that traces of a primitive arctic culture can be traced from the most northernly part of Norway, across northern Asia, over the Bering Strait and far south in North America. Heyerdahl's incomparble KonTiki expedition showed that certain elements of American culture may have reached Polynesia. Once cautious scientists now arrive at increasngly daring conclusions, especially with regard to the art of Mexico and that of the Far East (so daring that the similarities become proof of direct contact, an immigration of bearers of culture from China). Indeed, the similarities are sometimes so striking that it is difficult to deny the possibility of Asiatic cultural elements having reached the ancient cultures of Mexico.[33]

The question of arrival time for the first group in the New World is addressed in Robert Wauchope's fascinating studies:

There is still a wide range of informed opinion on the time of man's arrival in America. Dr. George F. Carter, a geographer, contends that man reached the San Diego area of California as early as 100,000 years ago. Dr. James B. Griffin, an archaeologist, although granting that a number of discoveries support the argument that man may have been in the New World some 20,000 to 30,000 years ago, does not feel that, as yet, any of them clearly demonstrate that this was no earlier than 10,000 to 12,000 B.C.[34]

The reader may wonder why the author offers so many references on the subject of Indian origins. This is done for the express purpose of helping us understand that evidence continues to mount regarding obvious cultural links between the Old and the New Worlds, anciently.

A colonial priest named Fray Diego Duran supports accounts of some ancient American records, with the following observation:

In order to discuss the real and truthful account of the origin and beginnings of these Indian nations, so mysterious and remote to us, and to discover the real truth about them, some divine revelation or spirit of God would be needed. However, lacking this, it will be necessary to make conjectures and reach conclusions through the many proofs that these people give us with their strange ways and manner of conduct and their lowly conversation, so like that of the Hebrews.[35]

Thor Heyerdahl's transoceanic crossing of the Atlantic, in 1969, proved that such ancient voyages were technically feasible. Other supportive studies indicate not only were these voyages possible, but actually did occur and are now being redomonstrated. It is Heyerdahl's opinion that there are enough evidences available now to confirm the theory that Middle America was the meeting ground for people or groups who crossed both the Atlantic and the Pacific Oceans.

For years, indications of pre-Columbian Nordic visitors to the New World have been mounting. Author Gloria Farley, long known for her exhaustive research on this subject, reported evidences which suggest contact between Norsemen and North American Indians in at least twenty-seven sites, in twelve different states.[36]

William Endicott, a *Los Angeles Times* writer, reported in the November 8, 1970 issue of the *Salt Lake Tribune,* that ancestors of the Melungeons—dark-skinned inhabitants of the eastern Tennessee bottom land—may have come to America 1500 years ago, finding their way across the ocean and then moving through North Carolina and Virginia to settle in the virgin Tennessee country.

Scientific analysis also has been applied to the task of determining racial links in the study of Indian orgins. Human cerumen (ear wax) occurs in two phenotypic forms—sticky (wet) and dry (hard). The consistency of cerumen is controlled by a single pair of genes in which the allele (heredity unit) for the sticky trait is dominant over the dry. Tests with 483 Indians from the North American tribes support the mongoloid (Asiatic) origin for the American Indian. However, these same tests in Chiapas, Mexico, indicated non-Mongolian ancestry for the Maya culture.[37]

3

Cultural Parallels Between
the Old and the New World

The idea of ancient contact between the Old and the New World has been studied and pondered repeatedly by writers, resulting in so many varying claims of origin, it appears there is no single root for this group we call the American Indians.

For years, scholars have enjoyed comparing one culture with another. Whenever a written history was not available, artifacts were the means by which authors and researchers were able to construct a possible story of an ancient civilization. Through this means, the persuasive power of comparison continues to increase the evidence linking the Old World with the Americas. Granted, three or four cultural parallels could be due to coincidence or chance. But, as the author has attempted an in-depth study of these similarities, personally visiting the major museums from around the world, over two hundred items common to both continents have been catalogued. This study, of necessity, had to follow over thirty years of the author's studying the cultures of ancient America—visiting, collecting data and photographing every major ruin and pre-Columbian civilization in North, Central and South America.

The emerging picture appears to be a multiplicity of contacts between the Old and the New World. In years past, most museums in the United States displayed maps indicating only one origin of the American Indian: the Bering Strait. Today, however, many major museums freely display charts and maps indicating the possibility of ancient marine navigation taking place on both the Atlantic and the Pacific oceans, with their travels originating in the Old World.

155

Of course, there are two opposing factions: (1) the Diffusionists, and (2) the Independent Inventionists. The *Diffusionists* attribute Old and New World similarities to land and transoceanic migrations of people between the Eastern and the Western Hemispheres. *The Independent Inventionists* maintain the many similarities are accidental, without contact, and thus ascribed as independent developments in the Old and the New World.

During the nineteenth century, an interesting idea developed regarding Atlantis, the island described by Plato as having been located in the Atlantic. Archaeologists suggested in 1967 the true Atlantis may be an island off the coast of Greece. It was supposed these people settled in both the Old and the New World. The island of Mu in the Pacific was also believed to have served the same purpose.[1]

As research continued, it became increasingly clear in scholarly circles that civilizations of the New World greatly resembled those of the Old. The major question became: "Could all these vast numbers of cultural similarities be due to accidental and independent development, or are they the result of ancient contacts and trade between the two major continents?"

The Diffusionist Viewpoint

After many years of research and study regarding the parallels or similarities between the old and the New Worlds, anciently, the author has joined those who believe in the Diffusionist theory. This decision was not solely due to book-study and available photographic comparisons, but also came through two personal research trips around the world, carefully cataloging data and photographing artifacts which draw on the dramatic similarities between the cultures of these two widely-separated continents.

Reed boat, bas-relief, ancient Egypt (Lionel casson, et al., ed., Joseph J. Thorndike, Jr., Mysteries of the Past [New York: American Heritage Publishing Company, Inc., 1977], p. 13).

Reed Boats - Peruvian - Mysteries of the Past, p. 13.

Ancient highway, Appian Way, 312 B.C., Rome, Italy.

Ancient highway, pre-Columbian, circa A.D. 1000-1440
Lurin Valley Pachacamac, Peru.

The author, however, wishes to substantiate his findings with similar research and conclusions offered by others which might strengthen the Diffusionist stand.

Following his archaeological discoveries in Alaska, F.G. Rainey wrote: "To refuse Neolithic man the ability to cross the southern Pacific and to accept his ability to cross or penetrate this region is straining at a gnat and swallowing a camel."[2]

C.A. Borden was of the opinion that small craft could certainly survive a long sea voyage, and concluded, seaworthiness had little to do with the size of the boat.[3]

From the multi-authored publication, *Man Across the Sea,* Erik K. Reed supports the idea of oceanic communication. He quotes J.D. Baldwin, who said:

Certainly there is nothing unreasonable or improbable in the supposition that the countries on the Western Mediterranean. . .communicated with America in very remote antiquity; nor is it improbable that there was communication across the Pacific.[4]

J. Hornell agrees in his conclusion that rafts of Ecuador and of coastal Asia probably are connected genetically.[5]

It is now believed, of 60 japanese junks drifing into the Pacific, at least a dozen reached the American coast.[6]

Edwin Doran, Jr., in his writings, says there is no question the rafts could have crossed the Pacific, repeatedly, in appreciable numbers.[7]

According to A.V. Kidder, "The facts suggest the possibility of diffusion from Indonesia or Indochina across the Pacific sometime before A.D. 200—400."[8]

Continuing research also supports diffusion with examples of trans-Pacific and trans-Atlantic explorations, duplicating primitive conditions, and such as Thor Heyerdahl's excursion from Peru to Tuamotu, in the Pacific, on the raft, *Kon-Tiki,*[9] and sailing across the Atlantic in his *Ra II* craft, a re-creation of an ancient reed ship from South America.[10] Captain Eric de

Bisschop built a Polynesian double canoe in Hawaii to make a study of the effects of an ocean voyage in such a craft, and where the trade winds might take him. He went from Polynesia to Fiji, then Java—finally to Madagascar, Cape Town and Europe.[11]

On the idea of diffusion through oceanic travel, Clinton R. Edwards wrote in *Man Across the Sea:* ". . .from the standpoint of available nautical capabilities, ancient crossings of the Atlantic were entirely possible."[12]

Then, in Herbert G. Baker's Commentary in Edwards' book, he added: "Surely there cannot now be any question but that there *were* visitors to the New World from the Old World (or vice-versa) in historic and even prehistoric time before 1492. The big problem is whether these visits were at all significant culturally."[13]

Transoceanic contact from the Old to the New World also has gained the support of Dr. Gordon F. Ekholm and Dr. Robert Hein-Geldern, from the staff of the American Museum of Natural History, in New York City. They agree, for example, that the columns and balustrades of Chichen Itza in Yucatan, as well as the serpent motifs, are almost identical with those found in Java. They also note similarities in the thrones and lotus motifs of India and Mayan countries.[14]

The diffusion of the sweet potato is a subject of interest and controversy amongst botanists, as it could not have floated from Peru to Polynesia without rotting. Thor Heyerdahl quotes a prominent botanist, E.D. Merrill:

> This pre-Magellan occurrence of the sweet potato in Polynesia I would accept as proof that the Polynesians and their remarkable expansion over the Pacific Islands, actually did reach the western coast of America, and that some of these early voyagers did succeed in returning to their island homes.[15]

Constance Irwin analyzed racial characteristics found in pre-Columbian America, in *Fair Gods and Stone Faces:*

> . . .How to account for such a conglomeration (in America): an Egyptian sphinx, the Egyptian god Ra, an Asyrian style, and Negroid types—and in addition. . .a bearded face of Semitic aspect? Where else on the face of the earth were these once blended?
>
> Where else? In the ancient Orient, a term employed in scholarly convention to indicate the ancient Near East or the Mediterranean East. More specifically, in the Syro-Palestinian region, including Phoenicia, which linked together the great river valleys of Egypt and Mesopotamia and freepartook of the cultures nurtured by both.[16]

Archaeologist James A. Ford has suggested the oldest type of pottery know in the Americas ". . .may have been introduced on the coast of Ecuador about 5,000 years ago, by voyagers from Japan."[17]

Historian Alvin M. Josephy, Jr. wrote: "Certainly by at least 1500 B.C., Asians were capable of making long sea trips." Much later, perhaps as late as A.D. 500-1000, when the islands of Polynesia were first populated, other long-distance oceanic voyages may have been made in one or both directions between America and the Pacific islands.[18]

Botanists are of the opinion that cotton seeds were carried to America from Asia in the second millennium B.C. The wind and the birds have been eliminated as possible carriers. Constance Irwin suggests that a manned vessel was the only alternative:

> This much is certain: he came; civilized man from the Old World sailed across an ocean and landed somewhere in the general area where the higher American cultures flourished in pre-Columbian times.[19]

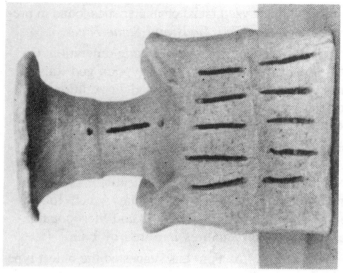

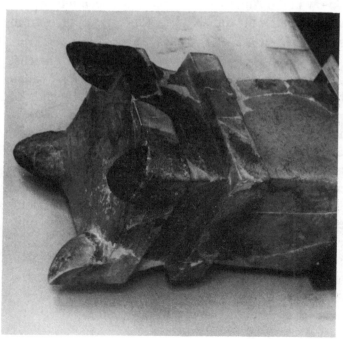

(Left) Horned altar, limestone, Megiddo, 1000 B.C., Rockefeller Museum, Jerusalem.
(Right) Horned Altar, pre-Columbian, Southern Mexico. (Thomas Stuart Ferguson, **One Fold and One Shepherd** [San Francisco: Books of California, 1958], pg. 87)

Other researchers have addressed the subject of burial practices, and also the mummies themselves, indicating white men
must have come to the Peruvian plain in very early times, but
Pierre Honore is even more emphatic: "...there is a stronger
evidence still, amounting to positive proof, from plant life, particularly cotton and the sweet potato, and possibly maize as
well."[20]

Phallic symbols found in Uxmal, near Merida, on the Yucatan Peninsula, cause speculation as to whether the people of
India made contact in the Americas. Hebrew and other Semitic
traits appear in the features of the American Indian, which again
raises the question of Old World ties.[21]

Following Columbus' discovery of America, Spain was the
only country among all the European powers attempting
conquests in the New World on a large scale. This, of course,
was partly due to existing European wars, which already had
drained the resources of other major powers.

From Adair's *History of the American Indians,* we learn the
first Catholic priests, who followed the Spanish conquerors to
this country, were amazed by the cultural similarities between
the people in the Americas and those of the Old World;
commenting particularly how the American Indians were very
much like the Hebrews.[22]

The theory of American Indians being the (lost) ten tribes
of Israel was also very popular at one time in colonial America.
For example, William Penn, wrote of the Indians of Pennsylvania:

I found them with like countenances with the Hebrew
race; and their children of so lively a resemblance to them
that a man would think himself in Duke's Place or Barry Street
in London, when he sees them....Their worship consists
in two parts, sacrifice and cantico, [songs]...They reckon

by moons; they offer their first ripe fruits; they have a kind
of feast of tabernacles; they are said to lay their alters with
twelve stones. . . .[23]

A. Hyatt and Ruth Verill also wrote of Old World roots in
America:

> Unquestionably the real truth is that man came to
> America from the Old World via all of these various routes.
> Some came from Europe by way of Greenland, others
> across the Atlantic to South America, some via the Bering
> Straits, and others across the Pacific. . . .[24]

Elsewhere in their work, Mr. and Mrs Verrill pinpoint an
exact people—the Sumerians—as being more like the people
of Peru than any other Near-Eastern people of whom we have
record:

> The results of Mrs. Verrill's work in conjunction with
> the author's first-hand knowledge of the ancient civilizations
> of Peru, would seem to prove conclusively that the pre-
> Incan civilization was brought to Peru ready-made and fully
> developed by Sumerian (Phoenician) explorers and
> colonists 2000 to 2500 B.C.[25]

Indeed, for ancient Hebrews to find their way to America
is well within the range of possibility. And, travelers from other
countries are also recorded. Charles G. Leland wrote of a
Buddhist monk who, in A.D. 400, sailed from China to America
and back in a Chinese junk.[26]

Joseph Needham also documents a fleet of 3,000 young men
and women who, in 219 B.C., sailed from China into the Pacific
ocean, never to return.[27]

Tongue and groove construction, the Temple of Amon-Re (1200 B.C.) Karnak, Egypt, near Luxor.

Tongue and groove construction, pre-Columbian, Temple of Tula, Tula, Mexico.

Corbelled arch, the Temple of Amon-Re, Karnak, Egypt.

Corbelled arch, pre-Columbian ruins of Kabah, Yacata. Mexico.

The Bat Creek Stone

Massive evidence, pro and con, valid and erroneous, has filled the pages of books and articles by professionals and amateurs, on the subject of Diffusion versus Independent Inventionists. What the diffusionists need now is a firm basis for their views such as an Eastern Mediterranean inscription, professionally excavated in an intact American archaeological setting.

Dr. Joseph Mahan thoroughly studied this type of literature in the late 60's, searching for just such an inscription recorded in the annals of American archaeology. After years of painstaking investigation, Dr. Mahan found record of a controlled study sponsored by the Smithsonian Institution at Bat Creek, Tennessee, in 1855-1856, under the supervision of Cyrus Thomas. Working their way down to the bottom of an "Indian" mound, Thomas and his crew found nine undisturbed skeletons, with an inscription partly under the skull of the main personage in the group. The sketch of the nine skeletons in the tomb and the photograph of the inscription, along with the report of the excavation were published by the Smithsonian Institution in 1894.[28] Thomas published the inscription upside down and presumed it to be Cherokee, although the writing bears no resemblance to the Cherokee syllabary. It remained for Dr. Mahan to turn the published photograph of the inscription *right side up* and recognize the characters as being in the ancient script of Canaan.

In August of 1970, Dr. Mahan sent Dr. Cyrus Gordon (an internationally respected scholar) a photograph of the inscription, from the stone itself (by this time deposited in the museum of the Smithsonian Institution in Washington D.C.) and requested Dr. Gordon's opinion as a Semitist. Dr. Gordon confirmed the text as being distinctively Jewish.

The circumstances surrounding the discovery of what is now known as *The Bat Creek Stone,* under the auspices of the

True arch, entrance to the birthplace of Jesus,
Bayt Lehm (Bethlehem).

True arch, pre-Columbian, entrance to Tomebamba,
Cuenca, Ecuador.

Post and lintel construction, ancient, Karnak, Egypt.

Post and lintel construction, pre-Columbian,
Tiahuanaco, Bolivia.

prestigious Smithsonian Institution, certainly rule out any suspecion of fraud, in this matter. The inscription confirms a migration of Jews from the Near East, possibly to escape the long hand of Rome after the disastrous Jewish defeats in A.D. 70-135. The author would classify this as an unimpeachable archaeological find, certainly strengthening the Diffusionist theory.

In his own writings, Dr. Cyrus Gordon elaborates on a stone found in Paraiba, Brazil, in 1872. For years scientists refused to accept the translations by a man who called himself "Joaquim Alves da Costa." It was not until 1967, that new light was shed on the Paraiba Stone through the work of Dr. Piccus, Professor of Hispanic Studies at the University of Massachusetts at Amherst. Dr. Gordon concluded after the more recent study, with increased knowledge, unknown in 1872, that ". . .the text is genuine. . .based on the fact that it contains readings unknown in 1872 but which are now authenticated by inscriptions discovered during the century that has elapsed since then."[29]

The Paraibal stone was found on da Costa's property near Paraiba (or Parahyba), broken into four pieces. No one understood the characters, but they were copied and mailed to experts, who contended and denied their authenticity until almost a century later. The text used Northwest Semitic inscriptions unknown in 1872 but now fully accepted. Dr. Gordon's translation of the stone is as follows:

> We are Sidonian Canaanites from the city of the Merchant King. We are cast up on this distant island, a land of mountains. . .and embarked from Eziongeber into the Red Sea. We voyaged with ten ships and were at sea together for two years around Africa. . . .So we have come here, twelve men and three women, into "Island of Iron."[30]

Dr. Gordon believes the voyage began in 534 B.C., and ended in Brazil in 531 B.C.[31]

It is interesting to note the word for "iron" in most Semitic languages is barzel, which is a Hebrew word. Dr. Gordon then comments:

> We can however say that no country in the world merits the name BRZL "Iron" more than Brazil, *whose chief resource is still iron.* Indeed it is reported that 25 percent of the world's known iron reserves are in the Brazilian province of Minas Gerais.[32]

Peter Farb wrote in *Man's Rise to Civilization* of the possibility of independent development of the Indians, but he also notes remarkable cultural parallels with the Old World, for which he offers no explanation. Farb's discussion of the Jamon culture in Japan, as compared with Equadorian Indian culture, is extremely interesting.[33]

Clark Wessler, noted for his research on the American Indian, writes of the American continent once containing elephants, horses, camels, and many other animals roaming its hills.[34] Wissler's contention is that these animals existed here before any human inhabitants appeared.

The Diffusion of Art

Middle American contact with Asia is a theory which had been argued by such scholars as Dr. Gordon F. Ekholm and Dr. Robert von Heine-Geldern. The late artist-archaeologist, Miguel Covarrubias, commenting upon the design of Maya objects of polished jade recovered from the depths of the cenote ("Well of Sacrifice") at Chichen Itza, said: "It would be hard not to share the belief in stronger and more direct ties with the East."[35]

The flowing vase was an early symbol in Bible lands, symbolizing one of the early astral myths, with its undulating streams flowing in opposite directions and considered as a "river of heaven." The undulating serpent became a symbol of that river. Regarded by ancient peoples as the seed or life-power of

*Flowing vase, pre-Columbian, circa A.D.
600 B.C. Zapotec, Oaxaca, Mexico.*

*Flowing vase in hands of goddess,
circa 2400 B.C., Iraq
(Ferguson, One Fold and One Shepherd, p. 80).*

Tree of life symbol. Stela 5 Izapa Stone, Izapa, Mexico.

Tree of life symbol, Old World, bas-relief, mirror handle, Hazor, Israel.

Eye-in-hand, Old World symbol, Jerusalem, Israel.

*Eye-in-hand, pre-Columbian, circular sandstone disk.
Moundville, Moundville, Alabama.*

(Left)
Fertility and love goddess Astarte, 700 B.C., Lachish
(Harry Thomas Frank, **Discovering the Biblical World**
[Maplewood, New Jersey: Hammond Inc., 1975], p. 125).

(Right)
Fertility goddess pre-Columbian, Museo de Cusco, Cusco, Peru.

*Triangle, hieroglyphic symbol, National Archaeological
Museum of Egypt, Cairo, Egypt.*

*Triangle, hieroglyphic symbol, cylinder seal,
600-300 B.C., Chiapas, Mexico
(Ferguson, **One Fold and One Shepherd**, p. 23).*

Double S glyph, symbol of clouds, rain and water, 1500 B.C.
*Old World, Asia Minor (Irmgard Grothe-Kimball, **The Art of***
***Ancient Mexico** [London: & Hudson Company], 1955).*

Double S glyph, symbol of clouds, rain and water,
*pre-Columbian, Teotihuacan, Mexico (Ferguson, **One Fold***
***and One Shepherd**, p. 92-93).*

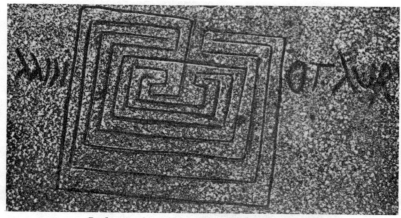

Labyrinth, A.D. 79, Knossos, Crete
(Barry Fell, American B.C.,) [New York: Quadrangle/The
New York Times Book Co., 1976], p.287).

Labyrinth, pre-Columbian, Oraibi, New Mexico
(Barry Fell, America B.C., p 287).

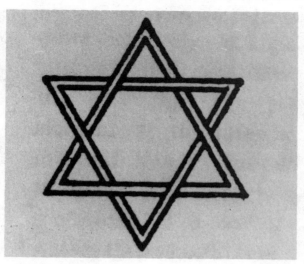

Star of David, interwoven triangles, ancient symbol of
Judaism, Palestine.

Star of David, interwoven triangles, pre-Columbian, circa
A.D. 731, Ceremonial center, Copan, Honduras.

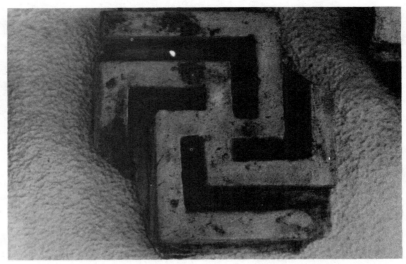

*Swastika from Priene, Greece, Antiken Museum,
room 14, West Berlin, Germany.*

*Swastika design, pre-Columbian jar, Museum of
Archaeology, Trujillo, Peru.*

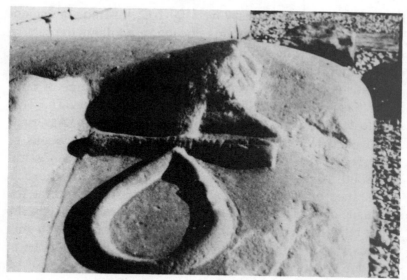

Life symbol, Temple of Amon-Re, Karnak, Egypt.

Life symbol, pre-Columbian, Ten Mile Canyon, Arizona.

deity, it was known as early as 2400 B.C., in Iraq. In ancient America, even the shape of this flowing vase follows the pattern of those in the Old World.[36]

Another shared symbol of Egypt and the Mayas was the serpent, hailed as the river of the sky and the source of rain, as well as a symbol of life, rebirth and resurrection. The Tree of Life design, found in ancient Sumerian, Egyptian, Assyrian, Hittite, and Hebraic cultures and mentioned in the books of Genesis and Revelation, may also be seen in Mexico, Central and South America. Dr. Matthew W. Stirling documented its appearance on a stele at Izapa, in Chiapas, Mexico, at the beginning of the Christian era. A Tree of Life design also appears in bas-relief on the lid of a sarcophagus in a chamber deep within the heart of a pyramid called the Temple of Inscriptions at Palenque, Mexico.[37]

The author has photographed an ancient Tree of Life symbol 600 feet in height, carved on a stone mountain facing the sea in Paracas, Peru. The people living there today still call it "the Tree of Life."

Old World Coins

Let us us also consider the subject of Old World coins found in the New World. Dr. Norman Totten, from Bentley College, Waltham, Massachusetts, has pursued research on ancient Old World coins found in America, and published extensively on his findings. Other material has come to light from our southeastern states through an accidental discovery. In the 1820's, John Haywood, Chief Justice of the Tennessee Supreme Court, gathered material for his book, *Natural and Aboriginal History of Tennessee*. In his findings, Haywood describes Roman coins found in Tennessee and adjacent states.[38]

And again on 17 April 1967, the New York Yiddish newspaper, *The Day-Jewish Journal, DER TAG*, Gershon Jacobson published an article on Hebrew coins of the Bar Kokhba

Rebellion, found by farmers near Louisville, Hopkinsville, and Clay City Kentucky. (See *Encyclopedia Judica* IV, p. 231.)

Then, to add to the diffusionist belief, John Fetterman published an article in *Life* magazine, 26 June 1970, in which he reported on the *Melungeons of Newman's Ridge* in eastern Tennessee. These people were neither Indians nor Negroes, but Caucasian, although not Anglo-Saxon as the other established white inhabitants of Kentucky. They were Mediterraneans, with their persistent traditions brought from the Iberian Peninsula to America, in Phoenician ships, about 2000 years before Columbus.[39]

Literary Styles

One of the more interesting parallels between the Old and New Worlds, anciently, is the chiasmus style of writing—a literary form with which we are all familiar in the Bible, in which we find a statement, followed by a *reverse structure of this same statement*. For example: "He that findeth his life shall lose it; And he that loseth his life for my sake shall find it." (See Matthew 10:39.) And again, "For my thoughts are not your thoughts, neither are your ways my ways, saith the Lord." (See Isaiah 55:8)

In the Book of Mormon, a book which reports three different migrations from the Middle East to the Americas between 2200 B.C. and 600 B.C., this same literary pattern is found, with the reverse form of the original statement:

And the Jews shall have the words of the Nephites, and the Nephites shall have the words of the Jews. And the Nephites and the Jews shall have the words of the lost tribes of Israel. And the lost tribes of Israel shall have the words of the Nephites and the Jews. (See Book of Mormon, 2 Nephi 29:13.)

A careful study of this interesting subject has been made by professor John W. Welch, in which he places the literary

Cylinder seals from Hazor, Israel, 2000 B.C.,
Archaeological Museum of Jerusalem, room 306, case #3.

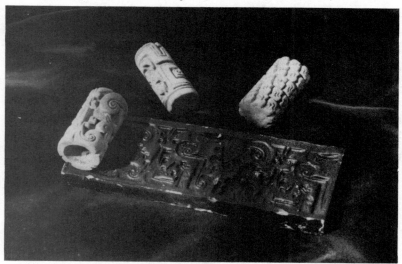

Cylinder seals, pre-Columbian, Mesoamerica,
Cheesman collection.

Writing on metal: Copper scrolls from the Dead Sea, 100 B.C., Qumran community. Khirbat, Qumran, Jordan Archaeological Museum, Amman, Jordan.

Writing on metal: Gold plate, pre-Columbian, Hugo Cohen collection, Lima, Peru.

Ring stamp seals, Egyptian, circa 1400 "v. Chr.," case VIb,
Museum of Fine Arts, Vienna, Austria.

Ring stamp seals, pre-Columbian, Mesoamerica.

Panpipes, Laos, #696, case 29,
Museum of Mankind, Vienna, Austria.

Panpipes, Vanuatu, New Hebrides (South Pacific), The
Bishop Museum, Honolulu, Hawaii.

aspects of the Book of Mormon as being on par with the Bible, with both books classified as great literary documents.[40] Again, two books with identical writing styles of scripture, from two different continents, is another point which certainly favors cultural diffusion. It is interesting to note, however, even though these writings indicate identical roots, somewhere in time, the Hebrew writers of the Bible were not even aware of the existence of the civilizations in the New World which produced the Book of Mormon, because of the vast oceans which separated the two continents.

In the Recinos-Goetz-Morley translation of the *Popol Vuh, the Sacred Book of the Ancient Quiche Maya,* we read,

In the province of Peten, to the south of Yucatan, the Spaniards, during their expedition of 1696 against the Itza, found some books written with characters which resembled Hebrew characters and also those used by the Chinese.[41]

John Lear describes the similarity of Minoan writing of the Old World with inscriptions found in ancient America on the Metcalf stone. He too concludes these inscriptions of a pre-Columbian tribe seemed to be linked culturally with the Hebrews of Biblical times.[42]

Musical Instruments

In *American Indians in the Pacific,* Thor Heyerdahl devoted an entire section of his studies to the diffusion of ancient musical instruments. He quotes a German author named E. Hornsbostel, who, in 1911, made a study of pan-pipes, and wrote:

In surveying the multiple forms of pan-pipes and their world distribution, one cannot overlook one strange fact, namely that the types of double rows—that is such as have an open pipe together with each closed one (of about the same length) to give the octave—only exist in two limited but widely separated territories: in the Solomon Islands and western Polynesia (Fiji, Samoa) on one side, and in Peru (even pre-Columbian) and Bolivia on the other.[43]

E. Nordenskiold, a Swedish writer, suggested in 1931, cultural exchanges could have taken place between South America and Polynesia, through a weather-driven Oceanic crew:

A culture element of this category may be the pan-pipe, which by many writers is considered to have been imported from Oceana. The pan-pipe occurs with the earlier ceramics in Nazca, and then in a highly developed form.[44]

According to Peter Farb, the pan-pipes of the Solomon Islands were also tuned to the same pitch and used the same scale as those in ancient America.[45]

Use of the single-note trumpet was far-flung, anciently, in many parts of the Pacific, and by the Inca and Quechua in South America. Also known as "conch trumpets," or "gourd trumpet," they were also used in ancient Crete and other Mediterranean cultures.[46]

Heyerdahl comments on the ancient slit drum—how parallel forms of the South American form are found in the Pacific, specifically Melanesia. He reports ". . .a very unusual form of foot-drum in a hole in the ground and stamped upon by the drummer. . .known from Easter Island and Hawaii, and is recorded from some North American Indians."[47]

In a monograph by K.G. Izikowitz (1935), the gourd rattle is considered: "Most likely we must look to Central America for the land of the origin of the gourd-rattle. . ." since these rattles were excavated from graves in ancient Peru. The use of gourd rattles in Hawaii is also recorded by Captain John Cook in his voyage to the Pacific in 1776-80.[48]

Thus we see that cultural diffusion may also have taken place from the Americas into the Pacific. Mankind is a curious lot. It has always been the nature of man to explore and learn of the mysteries beyond his boundaries. That they sailed into the

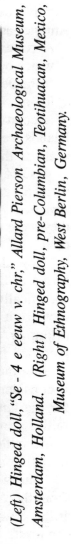

(Left) Hinged doll, "Se - 4 e eeuw v. chr," Allard Pierson Archaeological Museum, Amsterdam, Holland. (Right) Hinged doll, pre-Columbian, Teotihuacan, Mexico, Museum of Ethnography, West Berlin, Germany.

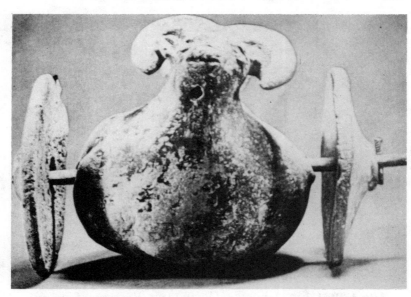

*Wheeled toy, "Ram on Wheels," circa 2300 B.C., indus region, northern India. (Eds. Time Inc., et al. **The Epic of Man** [New York: Time Inc., 1961], p. 90).*

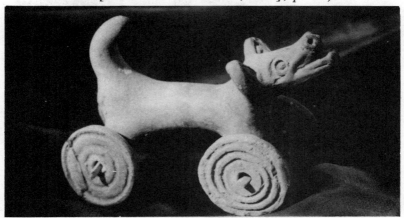

Wheeled toy, pre-Columbian, Mesoamerica, Stindahl collection.

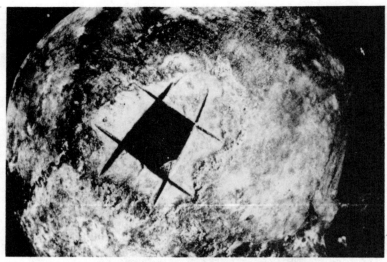

Skull trephination, Lachish, Palestine (Geofrey Ashe,
The Quest for America *[New York: Praeger; London:*
Pall Mall, 1971], pg. 122).

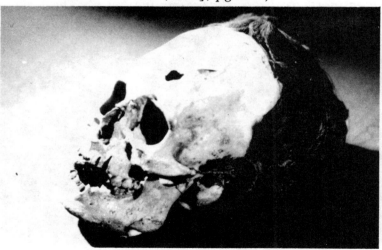

Skull trephination, Paracas, Peru, National Museum of
Anthropology and Archaeology, Lima, Peru.

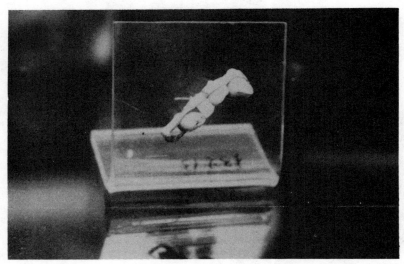

Dental work, gold braces on teeth, "praeneste," room 33,
National Museum of Villa Guilia, Rome, Italy.

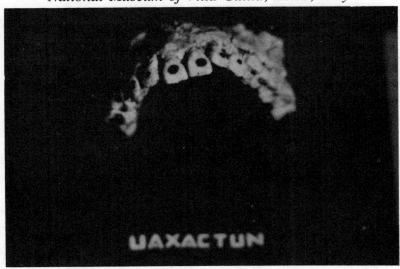

Dental work, pre-Columbian, Uaxactun,
Museum of Archaeology, Guatemala City, Guatemala.

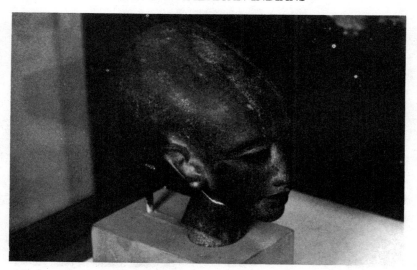

Head elongation, Egyptian princess, Antiken Museum, case #35, West Berlin, Germany.

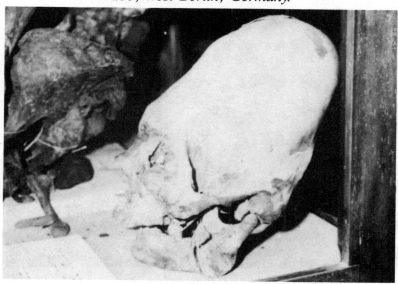

Head elongation, pre-Columbian, Museum of Archaeology and Anthropology, Lima, Peru.

Atlantic from the Old world to the Americas, and from the Americas into the Pacific, and vice versa, is perfectly possible.

Games
The rather sophisticated game of *parchisi* (also spelled *parcheese* or *pachisi*), which originated in India, is also found in prehistoric Mexico.[49]

Medical Practices
Skull surgery or trephining was practiced in the Stone, Bronze and Iron ages from Western Russia to the Atlantic Coast, as well as in distant Peru.[50]

Skull Flattening and Elongation
This practice was found in the Near East among the Armenoids (Armenia), and also among the people in Samoa, Tonga, the Marquesas, Fiji, and throughout Polynesia and again in Peru and Central Mexico. S. Griswold Morley wrote of depressed foreheads found in the New World cultures in his book, *The Ancient Maya,* indicating how they considered this deformation a mark of beauty. They would bind the heads of the babies, front and back, with boards, leaving them for several days. When the boards were removed, the child's head remained flattened for life.[51] It is the opinion of many archaeologists and scholars that this practice may have been an indication of rank or nobility.

Constance Irwin commented on this practice in Palenque, Mexico.

And here in the tomb of Palenque lies one accorded the title of god, a god with a crescent-shaped nose and a pointed beard—in fact, a god who could have passed for a native in ancient Phoenicia; for there too head deformation was practiced, as indeed it was practiced in may places throughout the fertile Crescent. Yahweh himself found it needful to enjoin the Hebrews: "Ye shall not round the corners of your heads."[52] (See Leviticus 19:27.)

Complete and circular deformation of the head was also practiced in Peru and Bolivia, and was also considered an aristocratic head-form.[53] In 1978, the author visited the Antiken Museum in West Berlin, and found (in case 35) the elongated head of an Egyptian princess, much like the rounded and deformed head of a skull which he photographed in the Museum of Anthropology and Archaeology in Lima, Peru, in 1968.

Physical Features

Author Earnest Hooton observed bodily features in the New World which would have been quite at home in Palestine.[54] And again, in Andrze J. Wiercinski's monograph on racial differences and similarities in the New World, he wrote:

...the ancient Mexican series are more shifted towards white variety patterns and facial traits than to the classic Mongoloids...ancient Mexico was inhabited by a chain of interrelated populations which can not be regarded as typical Mongoloids...features were introduced by [a] foreign band of sporadic immigrants from the Western Mediterranean area.[55]

Another point of interest is the incisor tooth (we often call it the fang) found in Asia, and also appears amongst the American Indians—deeply concave on the inner side, rounding on the outer edges in front, and slightly sunken in the center-front. The author's son, Dr. Ross A. Cheesman, a practicing dentist, calls this "a Navajo tooth."

Other Asiatic features which appear in several native American groups are the characteristic eyefold, and the pigmented spot at the base of the spine of infants.[56]

*Painted face on jar, circa 2500 B.C., Samarra culture, Mesopotamia (C.C. Lambert-Karlovsky and Jeremy A. Sabloff, **Ancient Civilizations: The Near East and Mesopotamia** [Menlo Park, California: Benjamin-Cummings Publishing Co., 1979], p. 97).*

Painted faces on jars, pre-Columbian, circa A.D. 1000-1300, Chancay culture, Peru.

Gold fingers, Egyptian, XXI Dynasty, Room 2, Case #14, National Archaeological Museum of Egypt, Cairo, Egypt.

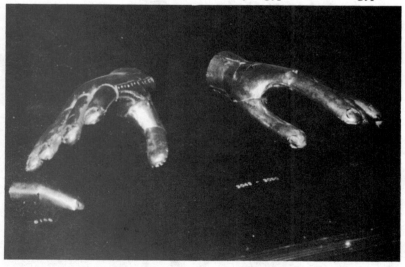

Gold fingers, pre-Columbian, Mujico Gallo Museum, Lima, Peru.

Hollow gold beads and pearls necklace, A.D. 600,
Louvre Museum, Paris, France.

Hollow gold beads, pre-Columbian,
Hugo Cohen Museum, Lima, Peru.

Royal headdress, horned and feathered, signifying "queen" or "princess," bas-relief, circa 500 B.C., Egypt.

Royal headdress, horned, stela 5 Izapa stone, Izapa, Mexico.

Racial Links

Belief that the ancient Americans were multi-racial is enhanced by Frenchman Paul Rivet's series, *Ancient Cities and Temples,* in which he speaks not only of the cranial deformation amongst the Mayas, but also of ". . .the prominent nose with convex bridge [land]. . .not very different from the Armenoid type from the plateux of Iran, with hooked noses and from the Alpine type with round heads."[57]

Even blood grouping studies in 1967, by G.A. Matson, concluded that ". . .a sensible position. . .is that the American Indians are not completely Mongoloid."[58]

The author is in complete agreement with Dr. Cyrus H. Gordon who classifies an Indian as any of the various groups existing in the Americas when Columbus arrived in 1492. These groups show such variation, beginning with the Mongoloid features of the Indians to the north, then.

In general the farther they live from the Bering Strait. . .the less Mongoloid they look, some of them possessing strikingly prominent noses, long heads or wavy hair, in contrast to the flat noses, round heads and strait hair that the typical Mongoloids have today.[59]

In 1968, the author did some extensive field research in Lima, Peru. While photographing and cataloging information on racial variations, he visited the home of a private citizen named Yoshitaro Amino, in Miraflores, Peru, who showed him a case of seven pre-Columbian portrait jars, the ancient counterpart of our photographs and portraits today—each seemed to be firmly identified as follows: (1) Greek, (2) Chinese, (3) Hebrew, (4) Negroid, (5) Arab, (6) Turkish, (7) Polynesian.

The author was also allowed to bring ancient American hair samples into the United States for academic study—from the burial mounds of Cajamarquilla, Peru. These ranged in colors from blond, to light brown, to red, to dark brown to jet black.

In plate XXXVI of Thor Heyerdahl's book *American Indians in the Pacific,* (between pages 320-321), he includes twelve full-color hair samples from the Museo Nacional de Antropologia y Arqueologia, in Lima, Peru. Eight of these hair samples are still on the skulls of the ancient dead—ranging in identical colors as those in the author's collection.

In Alexander Von Wuthenau's private collection is a bigger-than-life size long-headed, bearded Semite, so familiar to the Near East and resembling the Yemenite Jews. His nose seems to extend straight up to his forehead, in typical Maya fashion. Much of the ancient American art clearly indicates multi-racial groups such as Semitic, Chinese, and Black.[60]

One of Mexico's leading anthropologists, Dr. Juan Comas, was asked if the ancient Americans were a biological homogeneous group. He answered with a solid 'No!''[61]

Religious Practices

The further we go back into the history of mankind the more preoccupied they were with god and religion in their lives. Much of the great art, music, sculpture and architecture of the Old World was based on religious concepts and philosophies. And so it was with many of the early civilizations, such as the Olmec, Mayan, Egyptian, Assyrian, Babylonian and Phoenician—so similar in many aspects of their cultures.[62]

Clearly, baptism was understood long before Christianity of the New Testament times:

According to rabinnical teachings, which dominated even during the existence of the temple, baptism next to circumcision and sacrifice was an absolutely necessary condition to be fulfilled by a proselyte to Judaism.[63]

Certainly, the Christian world is comfortable with this idea.

William Sanford La Sor writes of the importance of the Jewish baptism by immersion—called *Miqva'ot* or *Miqveh* in

Baptismal font, Qumran community, Wadi Qumran (near the northwestern shore of the Dead Sea), Khirbat, Qumran.

Baptismal font ("sacred bath"), Pachacamac, Peru.

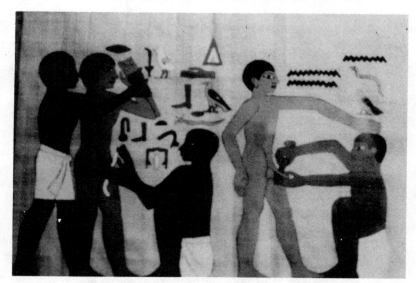

*Practice of circumcision, mural, Temple of
Oman-Re, Karnak, Egypt (Photograph: Dr. James Sullivan,
Columbus, Georgia).*

*Practice of circumcision, pre-Columbian, mural, Great
Pyramid at Teotihuacan, near Mexico City, Mexico.*

*Stone Buddha, "Granting of Wish" and "Granting of Courage"
gesture, circa A.D. 600, China, Freer Gallery of Art Washington,
D.C., (Paul Shao, **Asiatic Influences in Pre-Columbian Art**
[Ames, Iowa: The Iowa State University Press, 1976], p. 165)*

*Stone God of Maize, circa A.D. 700, Copan Honduras, Museum of Mankind, British Museum, London (Shao, **Asiatic Influences**, p. 166).*

Seated Buddha, circa A.D. 1400, Thailand
(Shao, **Asiatic Influences***, p. 87).*

Seated woman, pre-Columbian, circa A.D. 600-900,
Vera Cruz, Mexico, National Museum of Anthropology,
Mexico City, Mexico.

singular—immersion baths dating to the late Second Temple period, prior to and during the period of John the Baptist:

The ritual bathing pool was meant not for hygienic cleansing, but rather for ritual purification. . .in flowing water. . .Complete immersion was required. . ."Whosoever immerses himself must immerse his whole body, naked, and all of it at once. . . .And if any who is unclean immerses himself in his garments, the immersion still avails him since the water enters through the garments". . . .Even the hair must be totally immersed.[64]

In his research trips, the author has seen baptismal fonts beneath the early Christian churches in Ephesus, and the Church of the Annunciation in Nazareth, Israel. Baptism by sprinkling evolved much later, long after Christ's ministry with his original apostles.[65]

As we consider the practice of baptism amongst ancient Americans, Hebert Howe Bancroft, a prominent writer and historian quotes Shagun and other early chroniclers as saying that all people had to be baptized. He also adds this interesting information: the name given to this ordinance of baptism is *zihill*, which means *to be born again*.[66]

Baptism was a ceremony also practiced in the high American cultures. The Aztec ceremonially washed the child at birth and also four days later. The second time, a name was given. Later in life another baptism was performed and another name given. The Maya ceremonial sequence varied only in details from this. The Inca also baptized early in life, by immersion, and conferred a first name (later to be replaced) at the time of the rite.[67]

The author has reverified this information through his own research, finding a deep ancient baptismal font in Pachacamac, Peru, which was amazingly similar to the "sacred bath" found in Qumran, Israel.

Constance Irwin's comment is appropriate here:

On the other hand, it is hard to forget the vanguard of Spaniards who entered Mexico and Central America saw several things (including the rites of baptism and penance as practiced by the Mayas) which suggested to them that other Christians had passed this way before.[68]

What these early writers described certainly would serve as adequate evidence that some of these early Americans did at one time have and practice certain elements of Christianity as it is known today, including baptism.

The impact of Christ's (the great white god's) visit to the Americas was such that he is considered by historians to be the greatest single influence in the history of the New World in ancient times. Just as Christian history is dated before and after the birth of Christ, the Aztecs and their ancestors commenced their history with the appearance of the white god called Quetzalcoatl. Long before the arrival of the white man, gigantic pyramids and religious centers were erected to the memory of the bearded white god who visited them long ago and promised to return someday.[69]

Temples and Burial Practices

That many of the arts, crafts and temples of ancient America are very Egyptian and Hebraic in their styles has been the source of lengthy discussions and even a mystery amongst scholars. This is particularly so when we study their temples and methods of burial. When anatomist Sir Grafton Elliott traces all civilization back to Egypt,[70] one thinks immediately of how the Israelites were brought to live in the land of Goshen (see Genesis 46:33-34), when Joseph was sold into Egypt (see Genesis 37), then brought his father Israel and his brothers to live with him. From this point in time the Israelites became slaves to the Pharaohs (see Exodus 1:14; Exodus 6:5), producing their arts, crafts and pyramids until Moses freed the Israelites and took

Ziggurat pyramid, King Djoser, circa 2650 B.C., Saggara, Egypt.

Ziggurat pyramid, Chichen Itza, Mexico.

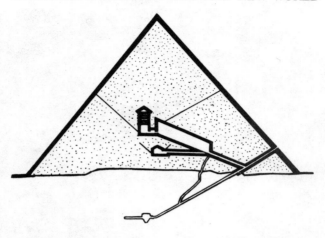

*Pyramid at Cheops, circa 2550 B.C., cross section, funerary chamber, Giza, Egypt (After sketch, Merly Severy, et al., ed. James B. Pritchard, **Everyday Life in Bible Times** [Washington, D.C.: National Geographic Society, 1967], p. 149.*

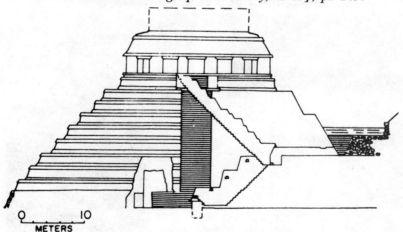

*Pyramid at Palenque, pre-Columbian, cross section, funerary chamber, Temple of Inscriptions. Palenque, Mexico (Gordon R. Willey, et al., ed. Robert Wauchope, Archaeology of Southern Mesoamerica, part one from the **Handbook of Middle American Indians** [Austin: University of Texas Press, 1964], p. 465).*

*Stone box—National Archaeological Museum,
Cairo, Egypt case D, #6089.*

*Stone box, pre-Columbian, Museum of Anthropology,
Mexico City, Mexico.*

*Carved figures, upraised hands, Sanci, India, 1st century A.D. (Ashe, **The Quest for America**, p. 249).*

Carved figures, upraised hands,
Chichen Itza, Yucatan, Mexico.

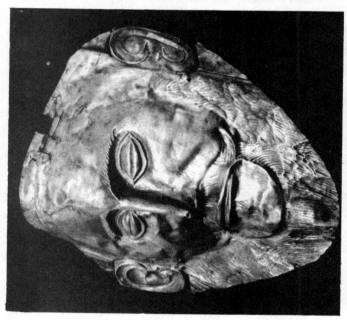

(Left) Gold mask, Mycenae grave, 1580-1500 B.C., main room, case #3, Archaeological Museum, Athens, Greece. (Right) Gold mask, God of Spring, Xipe Toltec, Monte Alban, Mexico, tomb #7. (Betty and Peter Ross, **Ancient Mexican Art** [London:Thames and Hudson, 1969], plate 134).

them back to the Promised Land (see Exodus 13:14). This background helps one understand the Egyptian-Hebraic influence in evidence throughout Mexico, Central and South America.

As we consider Old and New World temples and burial practices, we immediately see the parallels between their ancient temples. Dr. John Lundquist, a professor of religion and anthropology, wrote a dissertation in 1983 (University of Michigan), on typologies for ancient temples:

The temple is associated with the realm of the dead, the underworld, the afterlife, the grave....The temple is the link between this world and the next. It has been called "an antechamber between worlds."[71]

Archaeological evidence leaves little doubt that pyramids of Egypt served as funerary monuments for the early Pharaohs. This can also be said for similar structures in ancient America, such as the Temple of Inscriptions in Palenque, Mexico, and also a tomb found in the west quadrangle of Monte Alban, in Oaxaca, Mexico.[72] The author has also seen another princely interment beneath a pyramid at Tikal, in Guatemala, which sustains the Temple of the Red Stele—establishing the custom of pyramid burial in the lowland Maya area.

The architectural style of the stepped pyramid is exemplified by the famous Zoser's pyramid at Saqqara, Egypt. The stepped or Ziggurat pyramid is also found in the Tower of Babel—the most famous throughout the Old World—going back to the same period described in Genesis. One of the foremost Mexicologists, George C. Vaillant, compared the temple of Cholula, Mexico, as the counterpart to the Tower of Babel. Constance Irwin responds:

The striking physical resemblance between the pyramid of Cholula (in Pueblo, Mexico) and the Tower of Babel is augmented by an equally striking similarity between the Biblical account of Babel and the preconquest Mexican legend which entwined this largest American pyramid.[73]

Paul Shao, a Chinese author, has pointed out numerous art pieces which indicate Asiatic Influences in pre-Columbian America.[74]

When Alberto Ruiz investigated the Temple of Inscriptions in Palenque, Mexico, in 1949, he discovered a piece of flagstone on the floor underground, which appeared to have holes which might serve as fingerholds. Lifting up the stone they discovered a staircase filled with rubble much like those filling Egyptian pyramids. It took him and his crew 3 years to clear 68 steps, 65 feet below the main floor, eventually leading to a room containing a large sarcophagus (burial casket) 7 feet wide and 10 feet long, mounted on stone legs. The top was elaborately carved with the portrait of a man whose Mongoloid eyes and large nose identified him as a typical Maya. When the lid was removed they found the skeleton of a man who was obviously a great and distinguished leader. Every finger held a ring; his arms were covered with bracelets; he wore a beaded breastplate and his face was covered with a mosaic of jade. The stonemason carved a footed, flared and flattened base, very similar to those found in Egypt and Phoenicia.[75]

With this magnificient find by Alberto Ruiz, scholars were obliged to compare the purposes of some of the New World Pyramids as being similar to those of the Old World—that of being a suitable structure which could house venerated leaders in a manner befitting their position.

The similarities do not end here. Over the skeletal face were fragments of jade, esteemed by the Mayas as was gold to the Old World peoples. Likewise were deceased kings of Phoenicia interred with masks of gold, in the belief that the practice would protect them from maligning forces, after burial.[76]

Tools

In the archaeological museums of Lima, Peru and Mexico City, Mexico, the author has photographed and catalogued

Chisels, National Archaeological Museum of Egypt, Cairo, Egypt, room 9, case #78.

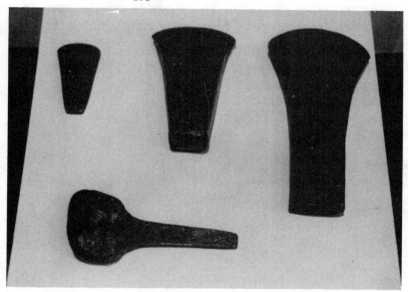

Chisels, pre-Columbian, Museum of Anthropology, Mexico City, Mexico.

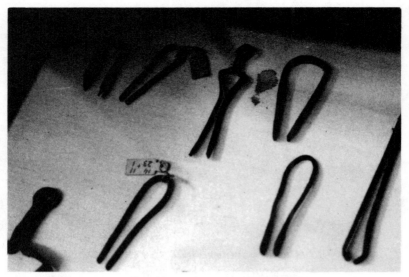

Tweezers, circa 3100-2700 B.C., Egypt, room 34, case #8, National Archaeological Museum of Egypt, Cairo, Egypt.

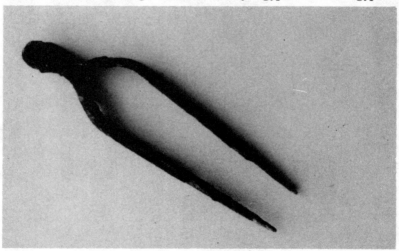

Tweezers, pre-Columbian, Peru, Cheesman collection.

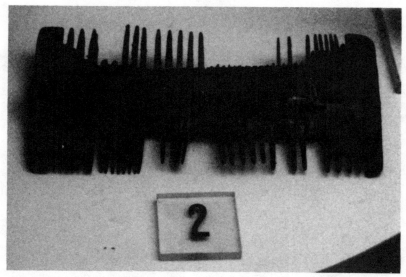

Comb, ancient, case 320 #2, Allard Pierson Archaeological Museum, Amsterdam, Holland.

Comb, pre-Columbian, Peru, Cheesman collection.

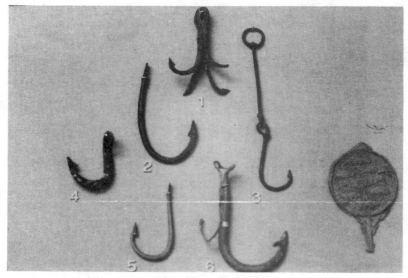

Six bronze fish hooks, Old World, Greek or Roman, British Museum, Great Russell Street, London, England.

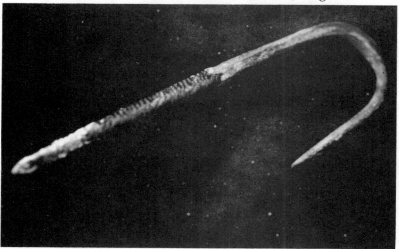

Fish hook, pre-Columbian, Lima, Peru, Cheesman Collection.

(Left) Balance scales, late Canaanite period (1000-550 B.C.), room 306, case #15, Archaeological Museum, Jerusalem. (Right) Balance scales, pre-Columbian, Peru, case #96, Museum of Mankind, West Berlin, Germany.

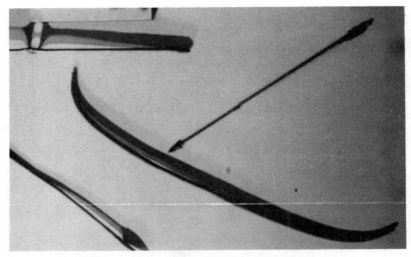

*Bow and arrow, case K, room #34, National
Archaeological Museum, Cairo, Egypt.*

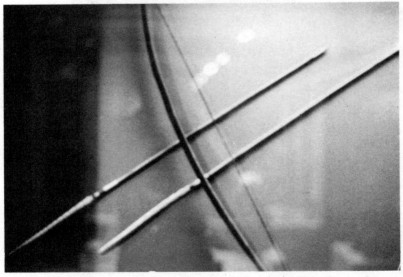

*Bow and arrow, pre-Columbian, Museum of Anthropology,
Mexico City, Mexico.*

Milling stone, Old World, Saudi Arabia.

Milling stone, pre-Columbian, Lima, Peru,
private collection.

ancient American chisels, hammers, tools for weaving, grinding, gears for simple machinery, and digging or planting sticks, which all have their counterpart in the Old World.

When Richard MacNeish wrote of *Early Man in the Andes,* he mentioned stone tools discovered in the highland of Peru which appeared to have cultural roots in Asia.[77]

William Prescott's *Conquest of Mexico,* written in 1843, presents invaluable translations of original documents of pre-Columbian datings, dealing with the conquest of Mexico and also revealing the moral character and customs of these remarkable ancient Americans. He speaks of the iron in their land but indicates it was used very little. Instead, they chose to make their tools of bronze, which could not only cut metals, but also the hardest substances such as basalt, amethysts and emeralds (with the aid of a silicious dust). Then an interesting comparison is made:

> Iron, however, was little used by the Ancient Egyptians, whose mighty monuments were hewn with bronze tools, while their weapons and domestic utensils were of the same material.

The early Americans also found a substitute for iron much like the Egyptians—an alloy of tin and copper, which is *bronze.*[78]

The ancients were also skilled in the art of working gold and silver. The early Spaniards admitted to the New World superiority in these ingenious works. Dr. Cyrus Gordon comments on this:

> However, the evidence for diffusion grows when an intricate complex, with numerous interlocking details, is involved. The extraction of metals by smelting ore might, in two widely spread cases, be due to independent development. But when we find in pre-Columbian America the sophisticated *cire perdue* ("lost wax") method of casting, long known in the Old World, it is more difficult to deny cultural diffusion.[79]

The Egyptians used a metate for grinding grain, exactly like those used in ancient America, and even today in isolated villages and settlements. The spindle whorl in the Middle East and Egypt also has its counterpart in the new world.

The hand looms of ancient Egypt are greatly similar to those used in the New World. Old and New World looms even have the same eleven working parts.[80] Even the cotton found in the burial mounds of Peru is ". . .a product of hybridizing the wild native American plant with Old World cotton such as was grown in ancient Egypt."[81] When one sees the beautiful samples of pre-Columbian textiles from Peru, as the author has, he would at once sense a cultural link to the ancient fabrics of Egypt and the Middle East. Dr. Cyrus Gordon puts it well:

Completely independent development is untenable because it would infer (1) an unexplained hybridization of Old and New World strains; as well as (2) the idea of spinning thread from the cotton boll; (3) the invention of the same types of looms; and (4) the application of the same weaving techniques for making the fabrics—all simultaneously in distant parts of the world completely out of touch with one another! Moreover the uses of the fabrics in Egypt and Peru include highly specialized applications such as mummy shrouds.[82]

The cotton boll certainly could not have floated across the ocean because water kills it, nor could birds have carried it because they won't touch the boll containing the seeds. It could not have been brought here by the Viking sea routes because it would not have survived the extreme cold. There is only one possible way it could have come—by an ocean vessel sailing the warmer seas.[83]

The author has in his possession (with permission, for academic study) samples of ancient American textiles from Peru, ranging from very plain homespun, to delicately embroidered

Metate, Saqqara, Egypt, room 47, National Archaeological Museum of Egypt, Cairo, Egypt.

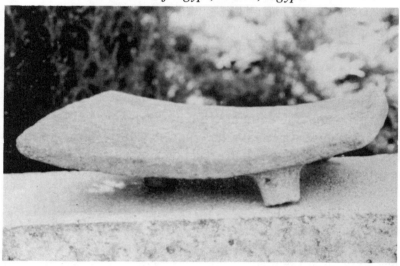

Metate, pre-Columbian, Costa Rica, Central America.

Spindle whorl, ancient, still used today, Memphis Egypt.

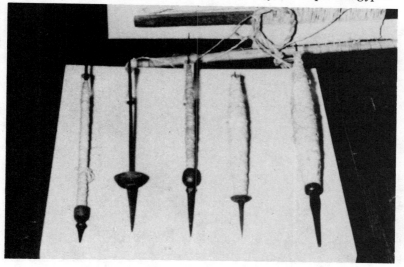

Spindle whorl, pre-Columbian, still used today, Peru,
Cheesman collection.

Weaving loom, Egyptian, 1897-1878 B.C. Museum of Fine Arts, Vienna, Austria.

Weaving loom, pre-Columbian, Museum of Archaeology, Trujillo, Peru.

borders, to multicolored woven figures with delicate threads, to the finest lace—the colors still bright after over 1,000 years!

Travel

Certainly there was inter-communication in the Americas, in pre-Columbian times, evidenced by similar cultural practices and art. Dugout canoes of considerable size were in pre-Columbian use in the Caribean, Central America, Ecuador, the Maya area, the Northwest Coast and parts of tropical South America.[84] One of these was seen by Columbus on his fourth voyage, and found to be eight feet wide, with twenty-five paddlers. The Maya carried on extensive trade with this type of vessel.[85]

Erland Nordenskiold writes of double-canoes in Peru, Central America, and Polynesia.[86] Actually the double-canoe was not always considered best for long distance travel by some Polynesians,[87] but it also was used on the American northwest coast, in Mexico, and in the Guianas.[88]

In 1970, Dr. R. Pocklington, from the Bermuda Biological Station for Research, supported the feasability of lengthy sea voyages anciently by documenting information gathered at the center, recording the arrival of an aboriginal group from Australia to the Americas.[89]

In a research trip to Polynesia, in 1974, the author visited the Museum of Archaeology, in Auckland, New Zealand. There in one of the wings was an enormous canoe as long as a good-size house. The curator told him the pre-Columbian canoe had the capacity to hold 100 people and (island hopping) travel a thousand miles.[90]

Then again, we might mention the record on the Metcalf stone (researched by Dr. Cyrus Gordon) found in the Americas, telling of a group of 15 people from Canaan who came across the Atlantic ocean in the 6th century B.C.[91]

Thor Heyerdahl's *Ra Expeditions* gave the world irrefutable evidence that it was perfectly possible to travel across the Atlantic ocean anciently, in a reed boat, which he reproduced for his controlled, scientific voyages—not once but twice![92] He also traveled across the Pacific Ocean in 1947, on the *Kon-Tiki* expedition, to disprove the then-current dogma that the aborigines from South America could never have reached the Polynesia.[93]

Indian Traditions

James Adair worked with the Indians for over forty years, during which time he kept a careful record of their oral traditions and tribal customs, publishing them in a very valuable *History of the American Indian*. The author wishes, at this time, to share some of the more interesting entries in Adair's book:

The Indian high-priest wears a breastplate made of a white conch-shell, and around his head "either a wreath of swan feathers, or a long piece of swan skin doubled," so as to show only the snowy feathers on each side. These remind us of the breastplate and mitre of the Jewish high-priest. They also have a magic stone which is transparent, and which the medicine men consult; it is most jealously guarded, even from their own people (Adair could never procure one).

Again, they have a feast of first-fruits, which they celebrate with songs and dances, repeating "Halelu-Halelu-Haleluiah" with great earnestness and fervor. They dance in three circles around the fire that cooks these fruits on an altar, shouting the praises of Yo-He-Wah. Hearing this. And, very much like the Hebrews of the Old World, they used this name in their religious festivals. (Adair did not mention the specific trip involved in the practice.)[94]

Then Adair offers the following reasons for his belief that some of the American Indians were descended from the Hebrew culture:

1. As the Israelites were divided into tribes and had chiefs, so do the Indians divide themselves; each tribe forming a little community within the nation.[95]

2. Hebrews worship Jehovah—Indians, Yohewah.[96]

3. Indians think Deity to be the immediate head of their state.[97]

4. The Jews believed in the ministering of angels, as do the Indians. They believe the higher regions to be inhabited by good spirits whom they call *Hottuk Ishtohoollo,* and *Nana Ishtohoollo,* which mean, respectively "holy people," and "relations to the great, holy one."[98]

5. The Indian language, and dialects, appear to have the very idiom and genius of the Hebrews.[99]

6. They count time after the manner of the Hebrews.[100]

7. After the manner of the Jews, the Indian Americans have their Prophets, High Priests, and others of a religious order.[101]

8. Festivals, fasts, and religious beliefs are similar.[102]

9. Hebrews offered daily sacrifice;...the Indians have similar religious services....The Indian women always throw a small piece of the fattest of the meat into the fire when they are eating, and frequently before they begin to eat. Sometimes they view it with a pleasing attention, and pretend to draw omens from it.[103]

10. The Hebrews had various ablutions and Anointings, according to the Mosaic ritual and all Indian nations constantly observe similar customs from religious motives.[104]

11. Indians have customs consonant to the Mosaic Laws of Uncleanliness.[105]

12. Like the Jews, the greatest part of southern Indians abstain from most things that are either in themselves, or in the general apprehesion of mankind loathsome, or unclean.[106]

13. The Indian marriages, divorces, and punishments of adultery still retain a strong likeness to the Jewish laws and customs.[107]

14. Indian punishments resemble those of the Jews.[108]

15. Indians had cities of refuge or places of safety, for those who killed a person unawares, and without design, similar to the Jews (see Numbers 35:6.)[109]

16. Before going to war, the Indians have many preparatory ceremonies of purification and fasting, like those of the Israelites.[110]

17. Choice and selection ornaments.[111]

18. Manner of curing their sick.[112]

19. Similarities in the burial of the dead.[113]

20. Mourning for the loss of deceased husbands.[114]

21. Raising seed to a deceased brother.[115]

22. The naming of children as best suiting circumstances and times.[116]

Banners

Banners existed among the Israelites at the time of their exodus from Egypt. During the exodus of the children of Israel from Egypt, each tribe is said to have had its own "standard, with the ensign of their father's house." (See Numbers 2:2; also chapters 2 and 10.) Apparently "the Israelites were the first to introduce national flags...since Israel was consecrated to the service of God...it was but proper that they should have also their banners corresponding to the colors of the precious stones...on Aaron's breastplate."[117] Tradition assigns a color, flag embroidery, and a precious stone to each tribe.[118]

Banners also existed in Mesoamerica. In describing the Aztec army, William H. Prescott wrote:

The Aztec princes...established various military orders, each having its privileges and peculiar insignia ....
The national standard, which has been compared to the ancient Roman, displayed in its embroidery of gold and featherwork, the armorial ensigns of the state. These were

*Banner, carried by Chinese soldiers, Angkor, A.D. 1296.
(Edward Bacon, ed.,* **Vanished Civilizations of the Ancient
World***, [New York: McGraw-Hill Book Co., Inc., 1963], p. 120).*

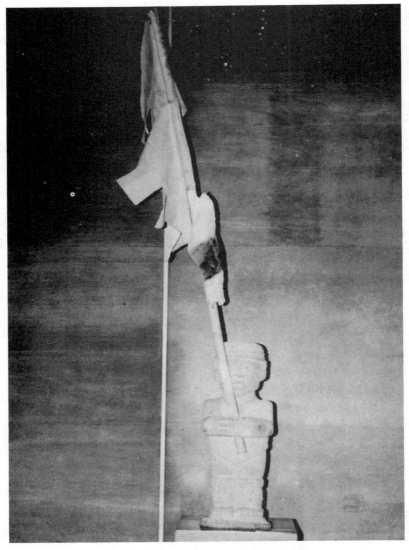

*Banner carried by one man, pre-Columbian, National Museum
of Anthropology, Mexico City, Mexico.*

significant of its name, which, as the names of both persons and place were borrowed from some material object, was easily expressed by hieroglyphical symbols. The companies and the great chiefs had also their appropriate banners and devices, and the gaudy hues of their many-colored plumes gave a dazzling splendor to the spectacle.[119]

Bernal Diaz del Castillo, in describing his expedition to Yucatan, wrote of the explorers coming to a stream on the coast "called the Rio de Vanderas or 'River of Banners,' " from the ensigns displayed by the same occurrence, quotes an eyewitness as saying the river was called "the Rio de Banderas, because we there came on a great number of Indians with long lances, and on every lance a great cloth banner which they waved as they beckoned to us."[120]

Prescot includes the following in the account of the 15 September 1519 *Encounter of Cortez,* and the army of the Tlascalan people who were said to be of Aztec stock:

Nothing could be more picturesque than the aspect of these Indian battalions. . . . The rear of the mighty host was dark with the shadow of banners, on which were emblazoned the armorial bearings of the great Tlascalan and Otomi chieftains. Among these, the white heron on the rock, the cognizance of the house of Zicotencatl was conspicuous, and, still more, the golden eagle with outspread wings, in the fashion of a Roman signum, richly ornamented with emeralds and silverwork, the great standard of the republic of Tlascala.[121]

Describing an artist's reproduction of an Aztec scene, Vaillant writes:

This procession of warriors show the imagination that governed gala dress. As this is a peacetime occasion, they are carrying flowers and standards in the place of weapons.[122]

These accounts indicate at the time of the Spanish conquest
of Mexico, the natives displayed colored banners with insignia.
The origin, exact description, and specific significance of the
banners remain to be researched. Speaking of the Maya, Villant
says the "colors had a strong ritualistic significance in Central
American religion."[123] yet, even that statement was not accompanied by further explanation.

Located in the Museum of Anthropology in Mexico City
is a statue of a person holding a banner. The pole and banner
have since disintegrated, but the positioning of the hands and
the hole cut into the stone indicate it was used to hold a banner
or flag.

Conclusion

Robert Wauchope, a well-known scientist, might summarize
the feelings of some diffusionists concerning the origin of the
New World civilizations:

> Perhaps the most popular theory about American Indian
> origins derives from the famous ancient civilizations of
> Mexico, Central America, and the Andes from Egypt.
> There were pyramids in both America and Egypt, there
> were mummies in Peru and Egypt, sun worship was
> practiced in many parts of the New World as well as in
> Egypt, and both areas produced hieroglyphic writing, royal
> tombs, bas-relief sculture, and a number of other similar
> customs and cultural traits. To most people the "archae-
> ology" conjures up but one picture: towering pyramids,
> the brood sphinx, King Tut's tomb, and the Valley of the
> Nile. it is only natural that when they see ancient relics
> like these somewhere else, even in faraway America, they
> see a connection with the classic expression of ancient
> civilizations—Dynastic Egypts.[124]

The idea of a common ancestry (but with resultant diversity of languages, tribes and cultures in Central America) was shared by Ignacio Bernal, former curator of the Museum of Anthropology, in Mexico City, in an interview with the author. The feeling of internationalism within Central America seems to be present also. The major traditions, however, seem to belong to one family, with varying language and dialects evolving through time.

In his book, *Before Columbus,* Dr. Cyrus Gordon credits Mesoamerica with setting the stage for the intermingling of Caucasians of Eurasia; Negroes from Africa; Mongolians from the Far East; and Phoenicians, Carthagenians, Egyptians, Greeks, Etruscans, Romans, and others from the Mediterranean. He details discoveries of modern archaeologists who confirm this belief. [125]

Following is a summary of his findings, which the author believes are representative of this particular research:

1. In the Early Stone Age, about thirty thousand years ago, waves of primitive Mongoloids came to America, across what is now called the Bering Strait.

2. Around five thousand years ago, pottery from the Jamon period in Japan appeared in Equador.

3. A Roman sculptured head dated about A.D. 200, was found in a controlled excavation by professionals in Mexico.

4. Off the coast of Venezuela a hoard of Mediterranean coins were discovered [reported by Mendel Peterson of the Smithsonian Institute], with so many duplicates that it cannot possibly be a numismatist's collection, but, rather, a supply of cash. Nearly all the coins are Roman, from the reign of Augustus to the fourth century A.D. It is the latter which gives us the *terminus a quo* (i.e., *time after which*) of the collection as a whole... It appears a Moorish ship, perhaps from Spain or North Africa, may have crossed the Atlantic around A.D. 800.

Stylized glyph on pottery, ancient China (Wei Chu-Hsien, China and America:
A Study of Ancient Communication Between the Two Lands. 2 vols. [Hong Kong:
Shuo Wen Publishing Co., 1970-71], I, plate 47, p. 41).

Stylized glyph on pottery, pre-Columbian
*(Wei Chu-Hsien, **China and America**, I, plate 59, p. 46).*

Bas-relief figure carrying satchel, from the palace of the Assyrian King, Ashwinasirpal (883-859 B.C.), room 19, British Museum, Great Russell St., London, England.

Bas-relief figure carrying satchel, pre—Columbian, La Venta, Mexico, outdoor Museum, Villahermosa, Mexico.

*Umbrella over important leader, bas-relief from the
Assyrian Palace (883-859 B.C.), capital city of Nimrod,
British Museum, Great Russell St., London.*

*Umbrella over important leader, bas-relief, pre-Columbian,
Stela 5 Izapa Stone, Izapa, Mexico.*

5. The Coimbra Map of A.D. 1424, shows portions of North America.[126]

In his book, *The Indian Heritage of America,* Alvin M. Joseph, Jr., wrote: "Certainly by at least 1500 B.C., Asians were capable of making long sea trips."[127]

Pierre Honore puts it beautifully:

. . .Crowns, thrones, litters, heraldic devices, standards; cups, plates, spoons and forks; the Bread of Heaven, baptism, confession, the blessing of the waters; the stories of the Flood and the Tower of Babel; it seems incredible that all these things were discovered and "invented" by the Indians. So they must have been brought in from the Old World by people who came to American shores very much earlier.[128]

John L. Stevens added his feeling concerning the Old and New World Link:

America, say historians, was peopled by savages; but savages never reared these structures, savages never carved these stones. When he asked the Indians who had made them, their dull answer was, "Quien sabe? (Who knows?)" There were no associations connected with this place, none of those stirring recollections which hallow Rome, Athens, and "The World's great mistress on the Egyptian plain." But architecture, sculpture, and painting, all the arts which embellish life, had flourished in this overgrown forest; orators, warriors and statesmen, beauty, ambition, and glory had lived and passed away, and none that such things had been, or could tell of their past existence. Books, the records of knowledge, are silent on this theme.[129]

Perhaps the reader might feel the author has belabored the point of diffusion and intercommunication between the Old and the New World, with quotes from so many sources. It is his desire to make the reader aware of the studies which have taken place—for more than a century—on this subject, and to help him feel confident that the world is no longer silent on this subject.

List of Cultural Similarites

And finally, the author wishes to conclude this chapter on Old and New World similarities and diffusion, with an alphabetical list of cultural similarities between the two continents. He has added to his own studies in this area, the contributions of Thomas Stuart Ferguson, Dr. John Sorenson, and others.

Some Major Cultural Similarities Between the Old and the New World

A

Adobe brick manufacturing
Altar (horned)
Angels
Anointing
Aprons
Aqueducts
Arch (true/corbelled)
Architecture of pillers
Arrowheads of metal
Artificial tears on Masks
Astronomy
Avocado

B

Balance scales
Ball courts
Banners
Baptismal font
Bark cloth

Beard (false and real)
Bearded men
Beaten sheets of metal
Bells
Bird man deities
Blood letting
Blood sacrifice
Blow gun
Bone ornaments
Bottle gourd
Bottle-shaped under-
     ground cistern
Bow and arrow
Breads (sacred)
Breastplates
Bucket (ritual)
Burial techniques
Burials
Burnt Offerings

C
Calendar system
Cannabalism
Caps
Carved steles
Casting by lost wax
Cement
Ceramics
Chickens
Chisels
Circumcision
Cities of refuge
Collars
Color representing
Colors (tribal)
Combs
Confession
Corbelled arch
Cotton
Creation story
Cross
Cup
Cylinder seals

D
Deity
Dentistry
Divorce
Drain pipes

E
Eagle and Serpent motifs
Ear plugs

Elders
Embalming with oil
Embossed designs on pots
Eye symbol

F
Fasting
Feathered headress
Feline
Fertility figurines
Festivals
Figurines holding up tables
Fishhooks
Flint blades of obsidian
Flood legend
Flowing vase
Flutes
Four quarters of the earth

G
Gold fingers
Gold plates (writing on)
Gourd

H
Hair types
Hand with eye
Healing of sick
Headdresses
Hebrew dialect and idiom
Helmet of Olmec
Hierarachic society
Hieroglyphs

High Priests
Highways
Horses
Holy water
Human sacrifice

I
Idolatry
Incense burners
Intentional deformation
  of skull
Irrigation

J
Jade carving
Jewelry

K
Knitting

L
Labyrinth
Life symbol
Lima beans
Lime plaster
Lintel construction
Loom
Lotus or water lily

M
Maces
Maize
Marriage

Mask (golden)
Mask (gold on corpse)
Mathematics
Method of naming children
Metal disc on roof of
  mouth of corpse
Metallurgy
Metate
Milling stones
Mirrors
Mosaic laws of cleanliness
Mosaic masonry
Motifs
Mourning the dead
Mummification
Mural painting
Musical scale
Musical instruments

N
Naming children befitting
  situation
Needles
Net fishing
Nose Rings

O
Obelisks
Observatories
Obsidian blades
Oil lamps
Overflowing vase motifs

P

Painting on pottery
Panpipes
Paper or writing surface
Parasol
Parcheesi game
Parchment
Petroglyphs
Phallic symbols
Pillars (half) as door
  frames
Plants
  Amaranths
  Bottle gourd
  Coconut
  Cotton
  Maize
  Peanut
  Pineapple
  Sweet potato
Plastic floors
Plating
Potters wheel
Pottery
Priesthood
Prophets
Punishment for adultery
Purification rituals
Purple dyes
Pyramid building (step)
Pyramid burial

Q

Quipu

R

Raising seed for deceased
  brother
Red dye
Reed boats
Ring seals
Roads
Rope
Rudder-oar on boats

S

Sacred purse/bucket
Sacrifice of doves and quail
Sacrifice (human and child)
Safe houses
Sandals
Sarcophagus of stone
Scales
Seer stones
Self mutilation
Serpent columns
Serpent with 7 heads
Seven-day time cycle
Shields
Short skirts for warriors
Sign (Double S)
Silk
Skull deformation
Slavery
Sling

Sphinx
Spindle whorl
Spoon, plate, tweezers,
  comb
Stamp seals
Stamps (flat)
Stela
Star of David
Stone boxes
Stucco
Sun dials
Sun worship
Swastica
Sweat rooms
Sweet potato

T
Tattoo
Temples and platform
Temple atop
Terrace agriculture
Textiles
Thrones
Time and seasons
Tomb under pyramid
Tongue and groove
  pillar construction

Tower of Babel story
Tree of life symbol
Trephination
Tribes and chiefs
True arch
Tweezers of metal

U
Umbrella symbol
Unleavened bread

W
Walls (double) with mud
  for insulation
Weaving techniques
Wheel toys
Women (pregnant holding
  breasts)

Z
Zero Concept

4

Conclusion

And so, the question is asked: What of these American Indians? They certainly originated from *somewhere!* Current studies indicate multi-racial origins for the Indians of the Americas. Clearly the age-old "all-came-over-the Bering-Strait" theory is no longer valid. As the author has pointed out in this volume, even blood types and cranial formations vary in many of the tribes, suggesting extremely cosmopolitan, multi-racial characteristics among our native Americans.

Their matchless ancient architecture, arts, crafts, textiles, and knowledge of science and engineering (following Old World patterns and forms), have all left the scholars and travelers breathless—a magnificent legacy for the world to admire, and certainly created feelings of justified pride among their decendants today.

In chapter one, the author has devoted an entire section to the prehistoric mounds and structures existing in North America, which might surprise some people who are convinced that major pre-Columbian ruins only existed in Mexico, Central, and South America. Cahokia Mounds, near St. Louis, Missouri, is a prime example of a major pyramid in the United States—larger than many of the pyramids in Central and South America.

And yet, today, the Indian groups no longer erect these marvelous structures and no longer live in the splendor which once existed here with their forefathers. When Columbus landed on the shores of the New World, he failed to find evidence of this once-glorious society. The Indians (as Columbus called them) were friendly, unpretentious people, living simply in their natural surroundings—functioning with a completely different lifestyle, compared to the sophisticated civilizations of some of their ancestors which the Spanish discovered centeries ago.

The United States government has tried to help them at times; at other times the government has treated them badly. Americans should not be proud of the history of treaties broken with the Indian groups. We are their guests. They were here first. Will they let us help?

There seems to be a great gap between their potential and what they have been allowed to accomplish today. What can we do to help them? Can we be more friendly to our fellow Americans? Can we promote workshops for developing skills and greater fellowship and trust? Can we create more cultural centers, where their fascinating arts and traditions can be preserved, and their talents and skills admired? Of course, a desire for education is at the heart of any progress, for anyone, not simply money alone. Knowledge is, and always has been the means of improving.

In conclusion, the author has presented research on two subjects: (1) the prehistoric peoples and civilizations of North America, and (2) the cultural similarities between the pre-Columbian civilizations of the Old and New World.

But the surface has only been scratched on these subjects. Much more research needs to be done on ancient American origins and the civilizations which once existed here. It is the author's earnest hope that in the years to come the field will be energetically pursued by others, and that their efforts will result in scientifice evidence which show the true origins of the ancient American Indians.

Ancient North American Cultures

Notes Chapter 1

1. Nelson A. Reed, "A Lost Indian Empire Found Six Minutes from St. Louis," *Argosy* (March 1971), pp. 47ff.

2. Stanley A. South, *Indians of North Carolina* (Raleigh: State Department of Archive History, 1970), pp. 26-33.

3. Franklin Folsom, *America's Ancient Treasures* (New York: Rand McNally & Company, 1974) pp. 120-21.

4. Delf Norona, "Moundsville's Mammoth Mound," *The West Virginia Archaeologist (Moundsville, West Virginia: West Virginia Archaeological Society, 1962).*

5. Delf Norona, "The Larkin Tablets," *The West Virginia Archaeologist* (Moundsville, West Virginia, 1950), Vol. II, pp. 2-3.

6. Edward V. McMichael, "Introduction to West Virginia Archaeology," *West Virginia Geological and Economic Survey,* 2nd ed. (Morgantown, West Virginia: State of West Virginia, 1968), p. 19.

7. James Ralph Skinner, *The Key to the Hebrew-Egyptian Mystery in the Source of Measures Originating the British Inch and the Ancient Cubit by Which Was Built the Great Pyramid of Egypt and the Temple of Solomon: etc.* (Cincinnati: R. Clarke & Company, 1875), p. 55.

8. McMichael, *op. cit.*, p. 2.

9. Martha A. Potter, *Ohio's Prehistoric Peoples* (Columbus: The Ohio Historical Society, 1968). pp. 41-42.

10. David Wyrick, *A Representation of the Two Stones* (Newark, Ohio: D. Wyrick, 1860).

11. This date was taken from the sign posted at the mound, erected by the Ohio Historical Society.

12. Charles Whittlesey, "Archaeological Frauds," *Historical and Archaeological Tracts,* No. 9 (February 1892), pp. 3-4.

Ancient North American Cultures

Notes Chapter 1

13. A.T.L. Beeston, *A Descriptive Grammar of Epigraphic South Arabic* (London: Luzac and Company, Ltd., 1962), p. iii.

14. Emerson F. Green, *Serpent Mound* (Columbus, Ohio: The Ohio Historical Society, 1970).

15. John P. Campbell, Ed., *Draper Collection, Border Forays, Draper Manuscript,* 3rd ed. (Wisconsin: State Historical Society of Wisconsin, June 1816).

16. John Locke, "Ancient Work in Highland County," A Second Annual Report on the Geological Survey of the State of Ohio (Columbus: The Ohio Historical Society, 1938).

17. Martha A. Potter and Edward S. Thomas, *Fort Hill* (Columbus: The Ohio Historical Society, 1970), pp. 33-36.

18. Folsom, *op. cit.,* pp. 136-37.

19. William H. Prescott, *History of the Conquest of Mexico* (New York: The First Modern Library, 1936), p. 694.

20. Albert James Pickett, *History of Alabama* (Spartanburg, South Carolina: Reprint Publishing Company, 1975), pp. 81-83, 88.

21. John A. Walthall, *Moundville, an Introduction to the Archaeology of a Mississippi Chiefdom* (Tuscaloosa: Alabama Museum of Natural History, University of Alabama, April 1977), pp. 17-19.

22. G.D. Pope, Jr, "Ocmulgee," *Historical Handbook Number Twenty Four* (Washington, D.C.: United States Department of Interior, 1961), p. 2.

23. "Slant Indian Village" (Mandan, North Dakota: North Dakota Park Service, undated).

Ancient North American Cultures

Notes Chapter 1

24. Albert R. Reagan, *The Sun God Moccasin Tales, Some Flood Myths of Indians,* 2 vols. (Provo, Utah: M.H. Graham printing Company, 1936), Vol. II, p. 133.

25. Folsom, *op cit.,* p. 133.

26. Ed. Phyllis Elving, *Southwest Indian Country* (Menlo Park, California: Lane Magazine and Book Company, 1974), pp. 5-6.

27. Brian and Jodi Freeman, *The Old Ones* (Albuquerque, New Mexico: The Think Shop, 1986), pp. 3-11.

28. Frank Waters, *The Book of the Hopi* (New York: Viking Press and Random House, Ballantine Books, 1963), pp. 37-38.

29. Edmund Nequataewa, ed. Mary-Russell F. Colton, *Truth of a Hopi* (Flagstaff, Arizona: Museum of Northern Arizona, Northland Press, 1973), pp. 128-29.

30. Douglas and Barbara Anderson, *Chaco Canyon* (Globe, Arizona: Southwest Parks and Monument Association, 1976).

31. Robert E. Ritzenthaler and Arthur Niehoff, *Famous American Indians* (Milwaukee Public Press, 1973), unnumbered.

32. *Ibid.*

33. *Ibid.*

34. Folsom, *op. cit.,* pp. 57-58.

35. These scaled models of early Indian dwellings were presented to Brigham Young University in 1983, by Robert J. Backstein, of Tacoma, Washington.

The Origins of the American Indian

Notes Chapter 2

1. J. Tuzo Wilson, *et al.*, *Our Continent* (Washington, D.C.: National Geographic society, 1976, p. 34.

2. Immanuel Velikovsky, *Earth in Upheaval* (New York: Doubleday, 1955; reprs., Laurel, Dell Publishing Co., Inc., 1968 through 1973), pp. 115-16.

3. Wilson, *Our Continent, op. cit.,* p. 30.

4. Andrew E. Rothovius, "The New Thing at Mystery Hill is 4000 Years Old," *Yankee,* XXXIX, No. 9 (September 1975), pp. 102-11.

5. Cieza de Leon, *The Incas of Pedro de Cieza de Leon,* trans. Harriet de Onis, ed. Victor Wolfgang von Hagen (Norman: University of Oklahoma Press, 1959), p. 273.

6. Fray Bernardino de Sahagun, Florentine Codex: *General History of the Things of New Spain,* trans. Charles E. Dibble & Arthur J.O. Anderson, 13 vols. (Santa Fe: School of American Research and the University of Utah, 1961), X, pp. 184-85.

7. *Ibid.*

8. *Ibid.,* p. 190.

9. Juan de Torquemada, *Monarquia Indiana* (Mexico City: Universidad Nacional Autonoma de Mexico, 1964), p. 15.

10. *ibid.,* p. 14.

11. Alfred Tozzer, *Landa's Relacion de las Cosas de Yucatan* (Cambridge: Peabody Museum, 1941) XVIII, pp. 16-17.

12. Adrian Recinos & Delia Goetz, eds., *The Annals of the Cakchiquels* (Norman: University of Oklahoma Press, 1953), p. 43.

13 Milton R. Hunter and Thomas Stuart Ferguson, *Ancient America and the Book of Mormon* (Oakland: Kolob Book Company, 1950), p. 25.

The Origins of the American Indian

Notes Chapter 2

14. *Ibid.*, p. 206.

15. *Ibid.*, p. 19-20.

16. *Ibid.*, p. 25.

17. A.R.Pagden, *Hernando Cortez* (New York: Orion Grossman, 1971), pp. 85-86.

18. Zelia Nuttall, "Some Unsolved Problems in Mexican Archaeology," *American Anthropologist* (N.S.), VIII (1906), p. 136.

19. Hernando Cortez, *Five Letters 1519-1529* (London: Routledge, 1928), p. 91.

20. R.A. Jairazbhoy, *Asians in Pre-Columbian Mexico: Old World Origins of American Civilizations* (Northwood: R.A. Jairazbhoy, 1976), II, p. 16.

21. *Ibid.*, p. 13.

22. Mary Corde Lorang, *Footloose Scientist in Mayan America* (New York: Scribner, 1966), pp. 270-80.

23. L. Sprague de Camp & Catherine C. de Camp, *Ancient Ruins and Archaeology,* (Garden City: Doubleday, 1946; repr. 1964), p. 167.

24. Harold Osborne, *South American Mythology* (Feltham, Middlesex: The Hamlyn Publishing Group Ltd., 1968), p. 61.

25. Guy E. Powell, *Latest Aztec Discoveries* (San Antonio: Naylor Co., 1967), p. 45.

26. Francis C. Kelley, *Blood Drenched Altars* (Milwaukee: The Bruce Publishing Company, 1935), pp. 32-33.

27. Charles Reginald Enock, *Mexico* (New York: Scribner, 1909-1910), p. 21.

The Origins of the American Indian

Notes Chapter 2

28. Sidney B. Sperry, *Science, Tradition and the Book of Mormon,* Salt Lake City: General Boards of MIA of The Church of Jesus Christ of Latter-day Saints, 1937), pp. 64-65.

29. Frank Waters, *Book of the Hopi* (New York: Viking Press, 1963), p. 31.

30. Lewis Spence, *Myths and Legends: The North American Indians* (Boston: David D. Nickerson, 1932), p. 41.

31. James Adair, *The History of the American Indians* (New York: Johnson Reprint Company, 1968), p. 22

32. Hubert Howe Bancroft, *The Native Races of the Pacific States of North America,* 5 vols. (San Francisco: D. Appleton Co., 1875-1883), V, p. 22.

33. Sigvald Linne, *Treasures of Mexican Art* (Stockholm: Nordisk Rotogravyr, 1956), p. 14.

34. Robert Wauchope, *Lost Tribes and Sunken Continents: Myths and Methods in the Study of American Indians* (Chicago: University of Chicago Press, 1962), p. 84, note 1.

35. Doris Heyden & Fernando Horcasites, *The Aztecs—The History of the Indies of New Spain.* (New York: Orion, 1964), p. 3.

36. Gloria Farley, "Pre-Columbian Norse and Indian Contacts," unpublished paper in author's possession, P.O. Box 84, Heavener, Oklahoma, 74937, 1974.

37. Nicolas L. Petrakis, Kathryn T. Molohom & David J. Tipper, "Cerumen in American India, and Genetic Implications of Sticky and Dry Types." *Science,* CLVII (December, 1967), pp. 1192-93.

Cultural Parallels Between the Old and the New World

Notes Chapter 3

1. Dana F. Kellerman, et al., eds., *The Living Webster Encyclopedic Dictionary of the English Language,* 5th ed. (Chicago: the English Language Institute of America, 1977), p. 63.

2. F.G. Riney, "The Significance of Recent Archaeological Discoveries in Inland Alaska," *Memoirs of the Society for American Archaeology,* No. 9, p. 46, supplement to *American Antiquity,* No. 18, pp.43-46, 1953.

3. C.A. Borden, *Sea Quest* (Philadelphia: MacRae Smith, 1967), pp. 25, 164.

4. Erik K. Reed, "Commentary: Section I," in *Man Across the Sea,* Carroll L. Riley *et al.,* eds. (Austin: University of Texas Press, 1971), p. 11, citing J.D. Baldwin, *Pre-Historic Nations,* 1869.

5. J. Hornell, "South American Balsas: The Problem of Their Origin," *Mariner's Mirror,* 17 (1931), pp. 347-55.

6. C.W. Brooke, "Reports of Japanese Vessels Wrecked in the North Pacific from the Earliest Records to the Present Time." Procedures of the California Academy of Science, (San Francisco: Golden Gate Park 94118), vol. 6, pp. 50-66.

7. Edwin Doran, Jr., *Man Across the Sea* (Austin: University of Texas Press, 1971), p. 135.

8. Alfred V. Kidder, "South American High Cultures" in *Prehistoric Man in the New World,* eds., Jesse D. Jennings and Edward Norbeck (Chicago: University of Chicago Press, 1964), p. 465.

9. Thor Heyerdahl, *Kon-Tiki,* (New York: Garden City Books; also Garden City: Doubleday & Co., Inc., 1950).

Cultural Parallels Between the Old and the New World
Notes Chapter 3

10. Thor Heyerdahl, *The Ra Expeditions* (Garden City: Doubleday & Co., Inc., 1971).

11. Eric de Bisschop, *The Voyage of Kaimiloa: from Honolulu to Cannes via Australia and the Cape of Good Hope in a Polynesian Double Canoe,* trans. Mark Ceppi (London: G. Bell & Sons, Ltd., 1940).

12. Clinton R. Edwards, "Commentary: Section II," *Man Across the Sea,* (Austin: University of Texas Press, 1971), p. 299.

13. Herbert G. Baker, "Commentary: Section III, *Man Across the Sea,* p. 438.

14. Personal interview, 28 April 1984, New York City.

15. Thor Heyerdahl, *American Indians in the Pacific* (London: George Allen & Unwin, Ltd., 1952), p. 428.

16. Constance Irwin, *Fair Gods and Stone Faces* (New York: St. Martin's Press, 1962), p. 71.

17. Alvin M. Josephy, Jr., *The Indian Heritage of America* (New York: Alfred A. Knopf, 1973), p. 101.

18. *Ibid.,* p. 40.

19. Irwin, *op. cit.,* p. 281.

20. Pierre Honore, *In Quest of the White God* (London: Hutchinson and Co., Ltd., 1961), p. 143.

21. Author's field research: North, Central, and South America, 1955-1987.

22. James Adair, *The History of the Amercian Indians* (New York: Johnson Reprint Company, 1968), pp. 17-18, 38, 106-107; cf Samuel Cole Williams, *Adair's History of the American Indian* (Johnson City, TN: Watauga Press, 1930).

Cultural Parallels Between the Old and the New World

Notes Chapter 3

21. Ethan Smith, *View of the Hebrews,* 2nd ed. (Poultney, Vermont: Smith and Shute, 1925), pp. 107-108.

24. A. Hyatt Verrill and Ruth Verrill, *America's Ancient Civilizations* (New York: Putnam's Sons, 1953), p. 11.

25. *Ibid.,* p. 293.

26. Charles G. Leland, *Fusang; or, The Discovery of America by Chinese Buddhist Priests in the Fifth Century* (London: Curzon Press; New York: Barnes & Noble, 1973), pp. 25-26.

27. Joseph Needham, *Science and Civilization in China,* vol. 4, pt. 3 (Cambridge, England: University Press, 1971), p. 553.

28. *Report on the Mound Explorations of the Bureau of Ethnology in the Twelfth Annual Report of the Bureau of Ethnology to the Secretary of the Smithsonian Institution 1890-91,* (Washington, D.C. Government Printing Office, 1894), pp. 393-94.

29. Cyrus H. Gordon, *Before Columbus* (New York: Crown Publishers, 1971), p. 122.

30. *Ibid.,* pp. 124-5.

31. *Ibid.*

32. *Ibid.,* p. 119.

33. Peter Farb, *Man's Rise to Civilization* (New York: E.P. Dutton and Co., 1968), pp 212-15.

34. Clark Wissler, *Indians of the United States* (Garden City, New York: Doubleday and Co., 1966), p. 3.

35. Alma M. Reed, *The Ancient Past of Mexico* (New York: Crown Publishers, 1987), p. 8.

Cultural Parallels Between the Old and the New World

Notes Chapter 3

36. Bruce W. Warren, Thomas Stuart Ferguson, *The Messiah in Ancient America* (Provo: Book of Mormon Research Foundation, 1987), p. 138.

37. Reed, *op. cit.*, p. 11.

38. John Haywood, *Natural and Aboriginal History of Tennessee,* 2nd ed. (Nashville: George Wilson, 1823, repr. 1959), pp. 178-84.

39. John Fetterman, "The Mystery of Newman's Ridge," *Life,* vol. 68, #24 (New York: Time & Life, 26 June 1970), Reginal section unnumbered.

40. John W. Welch, "A Book You Can Respect," *The Ensign,* (Salt Lake City, The Church of Jesus Christ of Latter-day Saints, September, 1977), pp. 45-48.

41. Delia Goetz, Sylvanus G. Morley, trans., Andrian Recinos, *Popol Vuh, the Sacred Book of the Ancient Quiche Maya* (Norman: University of Oklahoma Press, 1950), p. 10, Introduction.

42. John Lear, "Ancient Landings in America," *Saturday Review,* vol. 53 (July 18, 1970), pp. 18-19.

43. Heyerdahl, *Indians in the Pacific, op. cit.*, pp. 672-73.

44. *Ibid.,* p. 673.

45. Farb, *op. cit.*, pp. 212-13.

46. Heyerdahl, *Indians in the Pacific, op. cit.*, pp. 674-75.

47. *Ibid.,* p. 676.

48. *Ibid.,* p. 677.

49. Harold Sterling Gladwin, *Men Out of Asia* (New York: Whittlesly House of McGraw-Hill, 1947), p. 323.

Cultural Parallels Between the Old and the New World

Notes Chapter 3

50. Sharon S. McKern and Thomas W. McKern, "Brain Surgery in the Stone Age," *Science Digest,* vol. 67 (1970), pp. 33-37.

51. Sylvanis Griswold Morley, *The Ancient Maya,* rev. by George W. Brainerd, 3rd ed. (Palo Alto: Stanford University Press, 1956), p. 163.

52. Irwin, *op. cit.,* pp. 104-105.

53. Heyerdahl, *Indians in the Pacific, op. cit.,* p. 315.

54. Gladwin, *op. cit.,* pp. 108-109.

55. Andrzej Wiercinski, "Inter-and Intrapopulational Racial Differentiation of Tlatilco, Cerro de las Mesas, Teotihuacan, Monte Alban and Yucatan Maya," *Actas, Documentos y memorias, Congreso Internacional de Americanistas.* I, (1970), pp. 234, 240.

56. C.S. Coon, *The Living Races of Man* (New York: Knoft, 1966), pp. 152-54.

57. Paul Rivet, "Maya Cities," *Ancient Cities and Temples.* trans., Maria Kochan and Lionel Kochan (New York: Putnam, 1960), p. 227.

58. G. Albin Matson, *et al.,* "Distribution of Hereditary Blood Groups Among Indians in South America, IV, in Chile," *American Journal of Physical Anthropology,* 27 (1967), p. 188.

59. Gordon, *op. cit.,* pp. 21, 29.

60. Alexander von Wuthenau, *The Art of Terracotta Pottery in Pre-Columbia, Central and South America* (New York: Crown, 1965, repr. 1969), p. 48.

61. "Son Los Amerindios un grupo Biologicamenta Homogeneo?," *Cuadernos Americanos,* No. 3 (1967), pp. 117-25.

Cultural Parallels Between the Old and the New World

Notes Chapter 3

62. Irwin. *op. cit.*, p. 158.

63. Eds. David Bridger, Samuel Wolk, *Jewish Encyclopedia* (New York: Behrman House, 1962), Vol. 11, p. 400.

64. *The Works of Hubert Howe Bancroft* (San Francisco: San Francisco History Company, 1887) vol. V, p. 682.

65. James A. Talmage, *The Great Apostasy* (Salt Lake City: The Deseret News, 1909), pp. 117-19.

66. Cheesman, *The World of the Book of Mormon,* p. 155.

67. William E. Gates, "Commentary upon the Maya-lzentat Perez Codex," Papers of the Peabody Museum of American Archaeology and Ethnology, Vol. 6, Harvard University, November 1910, pp. 59-60.

68. Irwin, *op. cit.*, p. 18.

69. Cheesman, *op. cit.*, pp. 30-39.

70. R. Sprague and Catherine de Camp, *Ancient Ruins and Archaeology, op. cit.*, p. 167.

71. Dr. John Lundquist, *Typologies for Ancient Temples* (Michigan: University of Michigan, 1983) Proposition II.

72. Cheesman, *op. cit.*, pp. 106-107.

73. Irwin, *op. cit.*, p. 59.

74. Shao, Paul, Asiatic Influences in Pre-Columbian Art. (The Iowa University Press, Ames, Iowa; 1976).

75. Irwin, *op. cit.*, pp. 87-89.

76. *Ibid.*, p. 94.

77. Richard S. MacNeish, "Early Man in the Andes" *Scientific American,* vol. 224, no. 4 (April 1971), p. 36.

78. William H. Prescott, History of the Conquest of Mexico, (New York: John W. Lovell Co., 1843), Vol. 1, p. 114.

Cultural Parallels Between the Old and the New World

Notes Chapter 3

79. Gordon, *op. cit.*, p. 145.

80. Irwin, *Fair gods and Stone Faces*, p. 298.

81. *Ibid.*, p. 280.

82. Gordon, *op. cit.*, p. 145.

83. *Ibid.*

84. Erland Nordenskiold, "Origin of the Indian Civilizations in South America," ed., D. Jenness, *The American Aborigines* (Toronto: University of Toronto Press, 1933), p. 263.

85. Frans Blom, "Commerce Trade and Monetary Units of the Maya," *Annual Report of the Board of Regents of The Smithsonian Institution,* (Washington, D.C.: Smithsonian Institution, 1934).

86. Nordenskiold, *op. cit.*, p. 263.

87. W. Ellis, *Polynesian Researches During a Residence of Nearly Eight Years in the Society and Sandwich Islands,* in 4 Vols.; [London: Henry G. Bohn, 1959] Vol. I, pp. 160, 165.

88. Harold S. Gladwin, *Men out of Asia,* citing G.H.L. Pit-Rivers, *Evolution of Culture,* p. 165.

89. R. Pocklington, "Letters," *Science,* Vol. 167, (St. George Island, West Bermuda, March 1970), pp. 1670-71.

90. Paul R. Cheesman and Millie F. Cheesman, *Early America and the Polynesians (Provo: Community Press, 1975), p. 66.*

91. Gordon, *op. cit.*, p. 89ff.

92. Thor Heyerdahl, *The Ra Expeditions* (Garden City, New York: Doubleday & Company, Inc., 1971).

93. Thor Heyerdahl, *Kon Tiki* (Garden City, New York: Doubleday & Co., 1956).

94. Adair, *op. cit.*, pp. 84, 86, 110, 111.

Cultural Parallels Between the Old and the New World

Notes Chapter 3

95. Ibid., p. 15.
96. *Ibid.*, p. 18.
97. *Ibid.*, p. 32.
98. *Ibid.*, pp. 35-36.
99. *Ibid.*, p. 37.
100. *Ibid.*, p. 74.
101. *Ibid.*, p. 80.
102. *Ibid.*, p. 94.
103. *Ibid.*, p. 115.
104. *Ibid.*, p. 120.
105. *Ibid.*, p. 123.
106. *Ibid.*, p. 130.
107. *Ibid.*, p. 138.
108. *Ibid.*, p. 146.
109. *Ibid.*, p. 109.
110. *Ibid.*, p. 159.
111. *Ibid.*, p. 169.
112. *Ibid.*, p. 172
113. *Ibid.*, p. 177.
114. *Ibid.*, p. 186.
115. *Ibid.*, p. 189.
116. *Ibid.*, p. 191.
117. Samuel Rappaport, *A Treasury of the Midrash* (New York: KTAV Publishing House, 1969), p. 130.
118. *Ibid.*, p. 131.
119. William H. Prescott, *History of the Conquest of Mexico*, 2 vols. (Philadelphia: Lippincott, 1893), Vol. 1, pp. 40-41).

Cultural Parallels Between the Old and the New World

Notes Chapter 3

120. Bernal Diaz Castillo, *The Discovery and Conquest of Mexico, 1517-1521* (London: Routledge, 1928, repr. 1933), p. 68.

121. Prescott, *op. cit.*, pp. 358-59.

122. George C. Vaillant, *Artists and Craftsmen in Ancient Central America* (New York: American Museum of Natural History, 1935) 388), p. 65.

123. *Ibid.*, p. 58.

124. Robert Wauchope, *Lost Tribes and Sunken Continents* (Chicago: University of Chicago Press, 1962), p. 7.

125. Gordon, *op. cit.*, p. 30.

126. *Ibid.*, p. 68.

127. Alvin M. Joseph, Jr., *The Indian Heritage of America* (New York: Alfred A. Knopf, 1968), p. 40.

128. Honore, *op. cit.*, p. 35.

129. John L. Stevens, *Incidents of Travel in Central America, Chiapas, and Yucatan,* 2 vols. (New Brunswick, New Jersey: Rutgers University Press, 1949), p. 79.

Bibliography

Adair, James. *The History of the American Indian*. New York: Johnson Reprint Company, 1968.

Bancroft, Hubert Howe. *The Native Races of the Pacific States of North America*. 5 vols. San Francisco: D. Appleton Company, 1875-1883.

Bisschop, Eric de. *The Voyage of Kamiloa*. London: G. Bell and sons, 1940.

Blom, Frans. "Commerce Trade and Monetary Units of the Maya," *Annual Report of Regents of the Smithsonian Institution*, Washington D.C.: Smithsonian Institution (1934), 423.

Borden, C.A. *Sea Quest*. Philadelphia: MacRae Smith, 1967.

Brooke, C.W. "Reports of Japanese Vessels Wrecked in the North Pacific," *Procedures from the California Academy of Science*. San Francisco: California Academy of Science, Golden Gate Park 94118, VI, 50-66.

Buchanan, Golden R. "Indian Traditions," *Improvement Era*, LVII, No. 4 (April, 1955), 241.

Castillo, Bernal Diaz. *The Discovery and Conquest of Mexico*. London: Routledge, 1928.

Cheesman, Paul R. *The World of the Book of Mormon*. Bountiful, Utah, Horizon Publishers & Dist., 1980.

Cheesman, Paul R. Monographs, personal files.

Cieza de Leon, Pedro. *The Incas of Pedro de Cieze de Leon*, trans. Charles E. Dibble & Arthur J.O. Anderson. 13 vols. Norman: University of Oklahoma Press, 1959.

Coon, C.S. *The Living Races of Man*. New York: Alfred A. Knopf, Inc., 1966.

Cortez, Hernando. *Five Letters*. London: Routledge, 1928.

De Camp, Sprague and Catherine De Camp. *Ancient Ruins and Archaeology.* Garden City: Doubleday & Company, Inc., 1946

Ellis, W. *Polynesian Research During a Residence of Nearly Eight Years in the Society and Sandwich Islands.* 4 vols. London: Henry G. Bohn, 1859.

Endicott, William. *Salt Lake Tribune, November 8. 1970.*

Enock, Charles Reginald. *Mexico.* New York: Charles Scribner & Sons, 1909-10.

Evans-Wentz. Y.W., ed. *Tibetan Book of the Dead.* New York: Oxford University Press, 3rd ed., 1975.

Farb, Peter. *Man's Rise to Civilization.* New York: E.P. Dutton & Company, Inc., 1968.

Farley, Gloria. "Pre-Columbian, Norse, and Indian Contacts," unpublished monograph, P.O. 84, Heavener, Oklahoma, 74937.

Fetterman, John. "The Melungeons of Newman's Ridge," *Life,* LXVIII, #24, June 26, 1970, regional section unnumbered.

Goetz, Delia and Sylvanus Morley. *Popol Vuh, the Sacred Book of the Quiche Maya,* trans. Adrian Recinos. Norman: University of Oklahoma Press. 1950.

Gordon, Cyrus H. *Before Columbus.* New York: Crown Publishers, 1971.

Haywood, John. *Natural and Aboriginal History of Tennessee.* Nashville: George Wilson, 1823.

Heyden, Doris, and Fernando Horcasites. *The Aztecs: The History of the Indies of New Spain.* New York: Orion Publishers, 1964.

Heyerdahl, Thor. *American Indians in the Pacific.* London: George Allen & Unwin, 1952.

Heyerdahl, Thor. *Kon Tiki*. New York: Doubleday & Company, Inc., 1950.

Heyerdahl, Thor. *The Ra Expeditions*. Garden City: Doubleday & Company, Inc., 1971.

Hornell, J. "South American Balsas: the Problem of their Origin," *Mariners' Mirror*, XVII (1971), 347-55.

Honore, Pierre. *In Quest of the White God*. London: Hutchinson & Company, 1961.

Hunter, Milton R. and Thomas Stuart Ferguson. *Ancient America and the Book of Mormon*. Oakland: Kolob Book Company, 1950.

Irwin, Constance. *Fair Gods and Stone Faces*. New York: St. Martin's Press, 1962.

Ixtlilxochitl, Fernando de Alva. *Obras Historicas*. 2 vols. Mexico City: Universidad Nacional Autonoma de Mexico, Instituto de Investigaciones Historicas, 1975.

Jacobson, Gershon. *The Day-Jewish Journal, DER TAG*, April 17. 1967.

Jairazbhoy, R.A. *Asians in Pre-Columbian Mexico: Old World Origins of American Civilizations*. Northwood: R.A. Jairazbhoy, 1976.

Jennings, Jesse D. and Richard Norbeck. *Prehistoric Man in the New World*. Chicago: University of Chicago Press, 1964.

Josephy, Alvin M., Jr. *The Indian Heritage of America*. New York: Alfred A. Konpf, Inc., 1973.

Kellerman, Dana F., *et al. The Living Webster Encyclopedic Dictionary of the English Language*. 5th ed. Chicago: The English Institute of America, 1977.

Kelley, Francis C. *Blood Drenched Altars*. Milwaukee: Bruce Publishing Company, 1935: affiliate of New York: Crowell Collier Macmillian.

King, Beth S. *New York Times,* June 16, 1975.

Kingsborough, Lord (Edward King). *Antiquities of Mexico.* 9 vols. London: Henry G. Bohn, 1831-1848.

Lear, John, "Ancient Landings in America," *Saturday Review,* July 18, 1970, pp. 18-19.

Leland, Charles E. *Fusang: or, The Discovery of America by Chinese Buddhist Priests in the Fifth Century.* London: Curzon Press; New York: Barnes & Noble, Inc. 1973

Linne, Sigvald. *Treasures of Mexican Art.* Stockholm: Nordisk Rotogravyr, 1965.

Lorang, Mary Corde. *Footloose Scientist in Mayan America.* New York: Charles Scribner & Sons, 1966.

Lundquist, John. *Typologies for Ancient Temples.* Michigan: University of Michigan, 1983.

MacNeish, Richard S. "Early Man in the Andes," *Scientific American.* CCXXIV, No. 4 (April, 1971), 36.

Matson G. Albin, *et al.* "Distribution of Hereditary Blood Groups Among Indians in South America, IV, in Chile," *American Journal of Physical Anthropology,* XXVII, (1967), 188.

McKern, Sharon S. and Thomas W. McKern. "Brain Surgery in the Stone Age," *Science Digest,* LXVII (1970), 33-37.

Morley, Sylvanis G. *The Ancient Maya.* Palo Alto: Stanford University Press, 1956.

Needham, Joseph. *Science and Civilization in China.* Cambridge, England: University Press, 1971.

Nordenskiold, Erland, *et al.* "Origin of Indian Civilizations in South America," *The American Aborigines,* ed. U.C. Jenness. Toronto: University of Toronto Press, 1933.

Nuttall, Zelia. "Some Unsolved Problems in Mexican Archaeology," *American Anthropologist,* (N.S.), VII (1906), 136.

Osborn, Harold. *South American Mythology.* Middlesex: The Hamlyn Publishing Group Ltd., 1968.

Pagden, A.R. *Hernando Cortez.* New York: Orion Grossman, 1971.

Petrakis, Nicolas L., Kathryn T. Molohon, and David J. Tipper, "Cerumen in American India, and Genetic Implications of Sticky and Dry Types," *Science,* CLVIII (December, 1967), 1192-93.

Powell, Guy E. *Latest Aztec Discoveries.* San Antonio: Naylor Company, 1967.

Prescott, William H. *History of the Conquest of Mexico.* New York: John W. Lowell Company, 1843.

Rainey, F.G. "The Significance of Recent Archaeological Discoveries in Inland Alaska," *Memoirs of the Society for American Archaeology,* IX, 46: supplement to American Antiquity. (1953), XVIII, 43-46.

Rappaport, Samuel A. *Treasury of the Midrash.* New York: KTAV Publishing House, 1969.

Recinos, Alfred and Delia Goetz. *The Annals of the Cakchiquels.* Norman: University of Oklahoma Press, 1953.

Reed, Alma M. *The Ancient Past of Mexico.* New York: Crown Publishers, 1987.

Reed, Erick K. "Commentary: Section I," *Man Across the Sea.* eds. Carroll L. Riley, *et al.* Austin: University of Texas Press, 1971.

Rivet, Paul. *Maya cities.* New York: G.P. Putnam & Sons, 1960.

Rothovius, Andrew E. "The New Thing at Mystery Hill is 4000 Years Old," *Yankee,* XXXIX, No. 9 (September, 1975), 102-11.

Sahagun, Fray Bernardino de. *General History of the Things of New Spain.* Salt Lake City: University of Utah, 1961.

Smith, Ethan. *View of the Hebrews.* Poultney, Vermont: Smith & Shute, 1825.

"Son Los Amerindos un Grupo Biologicamenta Homogeneo?," *Cuadernos Americans,* CLII, No. 3 (1967), 117-25.

Spence, Lewis. *Myths and Legends: The North American Indians.* Boston, 1932.

The Holy Bible, authorized King James Version.

Torquemada, Juan de. *Monarquia Indiana.* Mexico City: Universidad Nacional Autonoma de Mexico, 1964.

Tozzer, Alfred. *Landa's Relacion de las Cosas de Yucatan.* Cambridge, Massachusetts: Peabody Museum, 1941.

Vaillant, George C. *Artists and Craftsmen in Central America.* New York: American Museum of Natural History, 1935.

Velikovsky, Immanuel. *Earth in Upheaval.* New York: Doubleday and Company, Inc., 1955.

Verrill, A. Hyatt and Ruth Verrill. *America's Ancient Civilizations. New York: G.P. Putnam's, Sons, 1953.*

Warren, Bruce W. Thomas Ferguson. *The Messiah in Ancient America.* Provo: Book of Mormon Research Foundation, 1987.

Water, Frank. *Book of the Hopi.* New York: Viking Press, 1963.

Wauchope, Robert. *Lost Tribes and Sunken Continents.* Chicago: University of Chicago Press, 1962.

Welch, John W. "A Book You Can Respect," *The Ensign.* (September, 1977), 45-48.

Wiercinski, Andrzej. "Inter- and Intropopulational Racial Differentiataion of Tlatilco, Cerro de las Mesas, Teotihuacan, Monte Alban and Yucatan Maya," *Actas, Documentos Y Memorias, Congreso Internacional de Americanistas,* I (1970), 234, 240.

Wilson, Tuzo J., *et al. Our Continent.* Washington D.C. National Geographic Society, 1976.

Wissler, Clark. *Indians of the United States.* Garden City: Doubleday and Company, Inc., 1966.

Wuthenau, Alexander Von. *The Art of Terracotta Pottery in Pre-Columbian, Central, and South America.* New York: Crown Publishers, 1965.

Interviews

1. Yoshitaro Amino, Miraflores, Peru, 1968.

2. Alton Stumblingbear, Anadarko, Oklahoma, 1968.

3. Igancio Bernal, Curator, Museum of Anthropology and Archaeology, Mexico City, Mexico, 1969.

4. Leader, Old Oraibai, Arizona Indian group, 1972.

5. Ivy Berry, Hong Kong, China, 1973.

6. Carey Mountain, Ute Indian, Fort Duchesne, Utah, 1975.

7. Irvin Earl Newton, Montgomery, Alabama, 1976.

8. Hopi Indian Community, Northern Arizona, 1978.

NOTE: All photographs, except those identified, were taken by Dr. Cheesman.